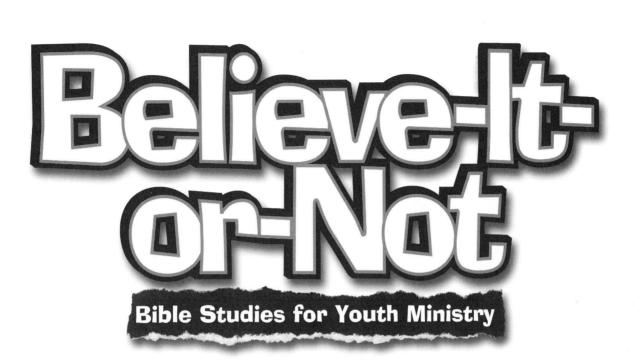

Believe-It-or-Not

Bible Studies for Youth Ministry

Group

Loveland, Colorado

www.group.com

Believe-It-or-Not Bible Studies for Youth Ministry

Copyright © 2000 Group Publishing, Inc.

Visit our Web site: **group.com**

Credits

Contributing Authors: Tim Baker, Karen Dockrey, Stacy Haverstock, Jan Kershner, Jim Kochenburger, Kelly Martin, Erin McKay, Julie Meiklejohn
Editor: Amy Simpson
Creative Development Editor: Jim Kochenburger
Chief Creative Officer: Joani Schultz
Copy Editor: Lyndsay E. Bierce
Art Director: Kari K. Monson
Cover Art Director: Jeff A. Storm
Designer and Computer Graphic Artist: iDesignEtc.
Cover Designer: Coonts Design Group LLC
Illustrator: Otto Pfannschmidt
Production Manager: Dodie Tipton

Library of Congress Cataloging-in-Publication Data

Believe-it-or-not : Bible studies for youth ministry.
        p. cm.
     Includes index.
     ISBN 978-0-7644-2218-8 (alk. paper)
     1. Bible--Study and teaching. 2. Church group work with youth. I. Title: Bible studies for youth ministry. II. Group Publishing.
  BS600.2.B43 2000
  220'.071'2--dc21   00-037625

14 13 12 11 10   12 11 10 09 08

Printed in the United States of America.

Contents

Introduction

So maybe the Bible doesn't top your teenagers' reading lists. They've heard all the Sunday school stories, and they think the Bible is nothing more than a collection of mild stories, neatly wrapped and tied with a bow. Been there, done that.

They're in for a surprise! Even young people who have grown up in Sunday school may not have heard—let alone studied—some of the more sensational stories in the Bible. Have they ever wrestled with why Jesus placed spit on a blind man? Have they ever tried to understand Ezekiel's incredible description of God? Have they ever wondered why God told a prophet to marry an adulterous woman?

Use these Bible studies to capture your teenagers' attention and to help them wrestle with some important questions. *Believe-It-or-Not Bible Studies for Youth Ministry* will remind them about God's power, protection, forgiveness, glory, and more.

These forty-five– to sixty-minute Bible studies present plenty of context and background information to help you and your students study the Bible in depth. Teenagers will be intrigued by the stories and, at the same time, challenged by the lessons they contain.

Use the Bible studies in this book to capture your students' interest in studying the Bible. You'll be helping them understand more about God in the process. Plus, you'll teach them to let the Bible take them by surprise.

An Unusual Messenger

Bible Study

Balaam's Donkey

Theme

God knows our hearts.

Scripture

Numbers 22

Supplies:

You'll need a slip of paper from the "Matching Motives" handout (p. 10) for each person, scissors, a bowl, a box filled with small items from around the house or the church, Bibles, paper, and pens or pencils.

Preparation:

Before this session, make enough photocopies of the "Matching Motives" handout (p. 10) for each person to have a slip of paper from the handout. Cut the handout apart where indicated, and place all the slips of paper in a bowl.

Gather some small items from around the house or the church and place them in a box—for example, a Bible, a heart cut from construction paper, a CD, a hammer, a screwdriver, and a pair of scissors. You'll need one item per person.

Study Numbers 22. Then read the entire session outline. Evaluate all the activities with your group in mind, and make any necessary changes.

Overview

This session teaches students about Balaam and how God made a donkey talk to reach him. It will help students remember that God knows our hearts and all our motives. Students will

~ define and discuss the word "motive,"

~ explore the difference between pure and impure motives,

~ experience the motives of the Bible story characters,

~ express willingness to have pure motives, and

~ respond in prayer.

Opener

As students arrive, have them form pairs, and ask each pair to discuss and define the word "motive." When everyone has arrived and has had a chance to create a definition, ask for volunteers to share their definitions with the group.

Say: **I really like the definitions you came up with. Today we're going to learn that God knows our motives and wants them to be pure.**

Ask:

~ **What do I mean when I talk about pure motives?**

~ **What makes a motive pure or impure?**

Say: **When our motives for doing something are impure, our actions can cause problems.**

Have each person take a "Matching Motives" slip from the bowl. Explain that each slip of paper has on it one of three statements that go together and that each person must find the other two people whose statements correspond to his or her own. Let them know that one statement must be an activity, the second must be a pure motive relating to that activity, and the third must be an impure motive relating to that activity. If you made more than one photocopy of the handout, some students will have identical statements.

After students have formed their trios, instruct them to discuss their statements and decide

Tell Me More

You may want to share this background information with your students to help them understand the story of Balaam's donkey.

Moab has an interesting history. It was formed by people with unusual origins. Lot's virgin daughters didn't want to die without having children, so they got their father drunk, slept with him, and had children. These babies were named "Moab," which means "from the father." These people settled east of the Dead Sea. Because they were considered outcasts, they had hard feelings toward Israel. God had ordered Israel to leave the Moabites alone, and Moses had probably let the Israelites know this. However, the Moabites wanted to ruin Israel if they had the chance.

which of the two motives is the right one, and why. Ask a volunteer from each group to share with the class. Say: **In every positive activity we do, our motives can be pleasing to God. Or we can do the right things with the wrong motives. That can cause problems. This is what happened to Balaam. God directed him to do something, and although he was doing what he was asked, his motives were all wrong. That caused Balaam some problems.**

Exploring God's Word

Have the class turn to Numbers 22 in their Bibles. Read the passage aloud to the group, or have students take turns reading a verse at a time. Say: **This is a pretty powerful story. The king of Moab came to Balaam and offered to pay him if Balaam would put a curse on the Israelites.**

Balaam wasn't a follower of God. He was a pagan who thought that he could manipulate God. When Balaam asked God to put a curse on the Israelites, God told him he wouldn't do it because the Israelites were a blessed people. But when Balak heard Balaam's answer, he sent more messengers promising Balaam a handsome reward for a curse on Israel. So Balaam went back to God and asked him again what to do. God told Balaam that he could go this time, but he was only to say what God directed him to say.

Balaam was very pleased and got on his donkey. But God was angry with Balaam because God knew what was in Balaam's heart. God saw that Balaam's motive for going to Moab wasn't pure. God knew that Balaam intended to curse the Israelites after all. Balaam didn't know God and didn't understand who he was dealing with. So God showed him by sending the angel.

Have students form four teams. Give each team paper and pens or pencils, and assign each team one of the following characters: the princes of Moab, Balaam, the donkey, and the angel. Direct each team to write a monologue, dialogue, or short skit about its assigned character. Teams must address what happened to each character in this Bible passage, the character's motive, and what the character may have learned from the experience.

After each team has prepared its scene, have students perform for each other. Lead the whole group in applauding after each team performs.

Then ask:

~ **What was each character's motive?**

~ **Let's look specifically at Balaam. Why was Balaam's motive impure?**

~ **How did God know Balaam's motive for going to Moab?**

~ **Why did Balaam's motive matter to God?**

~ **What was God's response to Balaam's impure motive?**

You may want to share this background information with your students to help them understand the story of Balaam's donkey.

Who was Balaam, anyway? According to Hitchcock's *Bible Names Dictionary*, his name means "the ancient of the people, or the destruction of the people." He was a man of some importance among his people, and he had a reputation as a successful prophet. It was because of this reputation that Balak sent for Balaam to curse Israel.

~ **How did God open Balaam's eyes to the impure motive?**

~ **After the donkey talked and Balaam saw the angel, do you think his motive was changed? Why or why not?**

~ **What can we learn from the story of Balaam's talking donkey?**

Say: **Sometimes God uses unusual means to open our eyes to the truth. In Balaam's case, God used an angel and made a donkey talk.**

Applying God's Word

Set out the box of items you previously prepared. Ask each person to secretly get an item from the box and then find a partner. Make sure students understand that their partners shouldn't see the objects they're holding.

Direct students to take turns playing Twenty Questions as they try to guess their partners' hidden items. In this game, one person answers questions asked by his or her partner. The questioning partner can ask only questions that can be answered "yes" or "no" in seeking clues to the object his or her partner is holding. Each person can ask up to twenty questions before the game is over.

Ask:

~ **How can we relate this game to our personal lives?**

~ **Why do we try to hide things?**

~ **Who do we hide things from?**

~ **How does God know our hearts?**

Say: **We learned from Balaam's story that God always knows our hearts. And God sometimes uses unusual ways to get our attention.**

Ask:

~ **If Balaam wasn't a follower of God, how did God know what was in Balaam's heart?**

Say: **God knows everything about everyone, even those people who don't believe in him. We can't hide anything from God. He doesn't have to play Twenty Questions to figure things out, either. He knows all the good and bad in our hearts that we hide from the world and sometimes even from ourselves. That's why in everything we do,** we should strive to have pure motives. We should seek ways to glorify God in every activity. Just as God knew Balaam's intentions, he knows our hearts!

Worship Time

Lead the group in the following responsive reading. After going through the reading once, encourage the group to create movements to go along with the words. Then repeat the responsive reading, using the movements students created.

Group: O God, make our hearts clean
Leader: So we can serve you.
Group: O God, make our hearts clean
Leader: So we can be made new.
Group: O God, make our hearts clean;
Leader: Make us more like you.
Group: O God, make our hearts clean
Leader: So we can serve you.

> ## Age Level Tip
>
> Have older teenagers form small groups and create new responsive readings for the whole group. They can use the words to a song or look in the book of Psalms for inspiration.

Say: **Isn't it amazing that even after all the times we've disappointed God, he still loves us? We sometimes get so wrapped up in the world and what it sees that we forget God sees the truth. He knows our hearts. He knows when we have clean and pure motives, and he also knows when we're doing things for all the wrong reasons. Remember that as you seek God, God will help you have a clean and pure heart—a heart that's pleasing to him, and one you won't have to hide.**

Closing

Ask the group to stand and pray with you by repeating after you.

Say: **Help us, O Lord, to seek you in all that we do.** (Pause.) **Help us recognize the need for pure motives in every activity.** (Pause.) **Help us remember that we can't hide anything from you.** (Pause.) **You know our hearts.** (Pause.) **Help us be honest with you and with other people.** (Pause.) **And make our hearts clean and holy.** (Pause.) **Thank you, Lord, for your love.** (Pause.) **In Jesus' name, amen.**

Matching Motives

ACTIVITY	PURE MOTIVE	IMPURE MOTIVE
Singing in the church youth choir...	to worship and glorify God.	to bring attention and honor to myself.
Attending church...	to learn about and worship God.	to find people to date.
Playing football...	to bring glory to God and share my faith with others.	to become popular.
Working a part-time job...	to learn to be responsible with money.	to buy lots of new clothes.
Doing homework...	to learn and do my best.	because there's nothing better to do.
Attending a school sporting event...	to have fun with my friends and share my faith with others.	to make out under the bleachers.
Getting involved in a school ministry...	to learn more about Jesus and be a leader at school.	because it will look good on college applications.
Going to a Christian concert...	to worship God and enjoy good music.	to make fun of other people who are having a good time.

Forgiving God, Forever Loyal

Bible Study
Ehud and the Fat King

Theme
God forgives.

Scripture
Judges 3

Supplies:
You'll need a nature videotape that explores nurturing behavior in the animal kingdom, a TV and VCR, Bibles, newsprint, colored markers, tape, paper, and pens or pencils.

Preparation:
Before this session, obtain a nature videotape that explores nurturing behavior in the animal kingdom, such as the parenting behavior of domestic or wild animals. Set up a TV and VCR, and make sure everything is working properly.

Study Judges 3. Then read the entire session outline. Evaluate all the activities with your group in mind, and make any necessary changes.

Overview
This session teaches students about God's faithfulness to his people despite their unfaithfulness to him. The Scripture focuses on a man chosen by God to deliver the Israelites from oppression by destroying the enemy—first through trickery and then through physical strength. Students will

~ discuss the experience of being ignored;

~ identify instances of human ignorance, disobedience, and subsequent need for help;

~ analyze the violence described in Judges 3;

~ examine ways they have ignored or disobeyed God and ways God has rescued them; and

~ compose rap songs to thank God for his faithfulness.

Opener

Have students form groups of three.

Say: **In your group, talk about a time in your life when you felt left out or ignored. Maybe your siblings ganged up on you. Perhaps all of your friends at school were talking about a movie you hadn't seen. Describe what happened and how you felt.**

After a few minutes, encourage volunteers to share their experiences with the entire group. Then ask:

~ **How did it feel to be left out or ignored?**

~ **What are some typical human responses to being ignored?**

~ **What is God's response to being ignored?**

Say: **Let's talk more about how God responds when people ignore or reject him.**

Exploring God's Word

Ask someone to read aloud Judges 3:7-15. Then write these four words on a piece of newsprint: disobedience, suffering, remorse, and rescue. Tape the newsprint where everyone can see it.

Say: **These verses describe a recurring pattern in Scripture, especially among the ancient Israelites. These four words illustrate the pattern I'm talking about. The**

Tell Me More

You may want to share this background information with your students to help them understand the story of Ehud.

Students may question how a loving God could allow, or even plan, the violence described in Judges 3. *Halley's Bible Handbook* provides one possible explanation: "God had founded a nation, for the purpose of paving the way for the coming of a Redeemer for the human race. God was determined to maintain that nation. And in spite of its Idolatry, and its Wickedness, God did maintain it." This viewpoint underscores the importance of sin (to God) and the necessity of salvation through Jesus.

people would disobey God, they would suffer the consequences, they would feel remorse, and God would rescue them.

Have each group spend a few minutes brainstorming about various scenarios that illustrate this same pattern. For example, one group might come up with the idea of two friends who swim beyond a boundary marker, get into trouble, call for help, and are then rescued by a lifeguard.

After about five minutes, ask groups to take turns pantomiming their scenarios for the rest of the group. After all the groups have performed their scenarios and the class has had a chance to guess what situations were being depicted, ask:

~ **In each of these scenarios, which characters most closely resembled God?**

~ **How does God's behavior make you feel about yourself? about God?**

~ **What generally needs to happen before God rescues us?**

~ **Why do you think God repeatedly rescues people?**

Next, have students form four new groups. Assign each group a different one of the following Scripture passages:

Group 1—Judges 3:16

Group 2—Judges 3:17-19

Group 3—Judges 3:20-23

Group 4—Judges 3:24-26

Give each group a sheet of newsprint and colored markers, and ask groups to illustrate their assigned verses. Explain that these "storyboards" must contain only pictures (no text). After five minutes, tape the storyboards where everyone can see them, and let the groups try to interpret one another's illustrations. Then, to make sure everyone hears the actual Scripture

Tell Me More

You may want to share this background information with your students to help them understand the story of Ehud.

Although we don't know for certain the significance of Ehud's left-handedness, it's possible that Ehud's right arm may have been useless due to some physical deformity or former injury. Whether this was the case or Ehud was simply left-handed by nature, it's possible that a blow from the left hand would have caught an enemy off guard. This detail may have been included in the story to show how God can turn our weaknesses into strengths or to illustrate that we can do all things through God, who strengthens us. Encourage students to search obscure details for important truths.

You may want to share this background information with your students to help them understand the story of Ehud.

Ronald E. Miller offers this question and commentary: "Is the pattern of Judges a recurring pattern in your life? Many Christians, even churches, depend heavily on the Lord when trials come, but live comfortably ignoring Him when life is going right. This is an up and down spiritual life, rather than a consistent mature walk with the Lord."

story, have someone read aloud Judges 3:16-26. Ask:
- **How do you think God felt about Ehud's murderous act? Explain.**
- **What was the "message" Ehud delivered to King Eglon by way of the dagger?**

Read aloud Judges 3:1 and Judges 3:27-30. Ask:
- **According to Ehud, who was going to help the Israelites defeat the Moabites?**
- **Why did the Israelites need to know how to fight?**
- **What was the result of all that bloodshed?**
- **Why do you think God allowed this violence?**
- **Who or what do you think is to blame for disharmony and violence in the world? Why?**

Say: **Even though people in this Scripture passage (just like people today) disobeyed God, God forgave them and rescued them. And he'll extend that same forgiveness to us if we ask for it.**

Applying God's Word

Ask students to remain in the four groups from the previous activity. Have students take turns talking about times they (or someone they know) experienced a pattern of disobedience, suffering, remorse, and rescue. After five minutes, ask a few volunteers to share their stories with the rest of the class.

Then ask:
- **In what ways does society ignore or disobey God?**
- **In what ways does society suffer because of people's ignorance or disobedience?**
- **When and how do you ask God for help?**
- **How does God rescue you?**
- **Why does God rescue you?**
- **What does today's Bible story imply about finding peace in your life?**
- **What does today's Bible story say about God's faithfulness?**

You may want to share this background information with your students to help them understand the significance of the book of Psalms.

According to *The Promise* (a "contemporary English version" of the Bible), "Psalms are poems that can either be sung as songs or spoken as prayers by individuals or groups. There are 150 psalms in [the book of Psalms], and many of them list King David as their author. They were collected over a long period of time and became a very important part of the worship of the people of Israel."

By sharing this definition of psalms with students, you will help them see that prayers can take many—even unexpected or unconventional—forms.

Worship Time

Distribute paper and pens or pencils to each group, and have groups compose letters to God according to the following assignments:

~ Working independently, each person in Group 1 will write a sentence describing how it feels to be separated from God.

~ Working independently, each person in Group 2 will write a sentence expressing remorse for ignoring or disobeying God.

~ Working independently, each person in Group 3 will write a sentence asking God for help with a particular problem.

~ Working independently, each person in Group 4 will write a sentence thanking God for his forgiveness and loyalty.

After several minutes, ask each student to read aloud his or her sentence, starting with students in Group 1 and ending with students in Group 4.

After everyone has read his or her sentence, give each group a Bible, and have each group choose a psalm about the recurring pattern of disobedience, suffering, remorse, and rescue. Then give groups five minutes to paraphrase, in rap format, the psalms they chose. Finally, ask groups to perform their rap worship songs for the rest of the class.

Closing

Show a portion of the nature video you selected. Then have students return to their four groups. Ask groups to identify and list any animal behaviors they saw that seem to reflect God's concern for us.

Age Level Tip

Some young teenagers lack the maturity to view birth, breast-feeding, and similar natural processes without embarrassment. Use discretion in choosing which video segments to have them watch.

For example, one group might list a bird's tireless efforts to feed its young, while another group might list a dog's patience with her playful puppies. After several minutes, have groups take turns reading their lists. Close with a prayer praising God for patience, forgiveness, and loving care.

Using the Unexpected

Bible Study
Jael and the Tent Peg

Theme
God can use anyone.

Scripture
Judges 4:1-10; 17-22

Supplies:
You'll need photocopies of the "Employee Profiles" handout (p. 22); paper; pens or pencils; newsprint; markers; tape; index cards; Bibles; craft supplies such as construction paper, newsprint, markers, glue, chenille wires, and yarn; a cassette or CD of soft instrumental worship music; and a cassette or CD player.

Preparation:
Before this session, make a photocopy of the "Employee Profiles" handout (p. 22) for each person.

Study Judges 4. Then read the entire session outline. Evaluate all the activities with your group in mind, and make any necessary changes.

Overview
This session teaches students that they don't have to be pretty or perfect or have it "all together" in order for God to use them. It reminds them that God wants to use them no matter who they are. Students will
- ~ talk about what makes people good candidates for jobs,
- ~ discover how God used Jael,
- ~ examine ways God can use them, and
- ~ commit to being used by God.

Opener

Give each person a copy of the "Employee Profiles" handout. Have students form four groups. Give each group paper and pens or pencils. Say: **You're part of an elite interviewing company. You've been asked to hire a computer salesman for a leading computer company. The computer company has narrowed their search to four pre-employment files. Your job is to sort through the files and choose the best candidate for the position.**

Give groups several minutes to review the personnel profiles on the handout and choose their candidates. When groups have chosen their candidates, ask them to prepare persuasive speeches to convince the rest of the class to hire the individual they have chosen. As groups begin to prepare their speeches, write the following questions on newsprint, and tape the newsprint to the wall where everyone can see it. Instruct groups to refer to these questions to help them prepare their speeches:

~ What, in your opinion, are this candidate's strengths?

~ What makes this person the best person for the job?

When groups are ready, gather the students. Say: **Now you have the task of hiring the right person for the job. I'd like you to seriously consider each speech you hear and do your best to make an unbiased decision when it's time to vote.**

Have groups present their speeches one at a time. Then give each student an index card and a pen or pencil and ask everyone to vote. When they have finished voting, tally the votes and announce the winner.

Ask:

~ **Which speech was the most persuasive? Why?**

~ **Did any of the speeches make you change your mind? Explain.**

~ **How can you be sure that this person will do the best job?**

~ **How can you tell who the right person is for any job?**

~ **How does God choose the people he will use to accomplish his will?**

Tell Me More

You may want to share this background information with your students to help them understand the story of Jael.

In the ancient Near East, men were customarily prohibited from entering the tents of women who were not their wives or daughters. Since no man could enter Jael's tent to search it, Sisera thought he had found an ideal hiding place!

~ **What kind of people does God use to accomplish his will?**

Say: **When God chooses people to accomplish his will, he doesn't always pick the most likely candidate for the job. Today I'd like us to look at the life of someone God used to accomplish his will, even though the person may not have been someone we'd choose.**

Exploring God's Word

Say: **God chooses unlikely people to do amazing things. Let's explore the story of one such person.**

Begin by reading aloud Judges 4:1-3.

Say: **This sets the stage for God to use someone we'd never expect in protecting the Israelites. The situation develops into an amazing event.**

Ask one student (or a few students) to read aloud Judges 4:4-10. Say: **There are some interesting things going on in this passage, and a lot of these things can be portrayed in pictures and shapes. I'd like you to work in your group to create a picture using the craft supplies I'll set out.**

Set out craft supplies such as construction paper, newsprint, markers, glue, chenille wires, and yarn. Give each group a piece of newsprint. Ask each group to use the craft supplies to create a mural, montage, or picture that depicts the events described in Judges 4:4-10. After several minutes, have groups present their creations. As groups present, have them share how their pictures relate to the passage.

Ask:

~ **What did you learn from looking at other groups' creations?**

~ **What was happening in this passage?**

~ **Why did God want Jabin's army to be defeated?**

~ **Why did Deborah tell Barak that the glory would go to a woman?**

~ **What was the most interesting part of this passage?**

Give each group paper and pens or pencils. Say: **If you'll look closely at this passage, you'll see God setting the stage to use someone that no one expected. Barak probably wanted the glory for defeating the army, but notice what Deborah said. She let Barak know that God would give the glory to someone else. I'd like you to stay in your group and read Judges 4:17-22. Then I'd like you to write what happened from Jael's perspective.**

Give groups several minutes to read the passage and write the situation from Jael's perspective. As they're writing, be sure to be available to groups that need help or more explanation.

After groups have shared their stories, have them form new groups of four.

Say: **We've looked at this passage a lot today. In your new group, I'd like you to share one thing you learned about the way God uses people we wouldn't expect him to use. As you're sharing, I'd like one of the people in your group to write down all of your responses.**

Give students several minutes to share within their groups. When they have finished, have groups share their lists with the entire class.

Applying God's Word

Say: **Have you ever thought about the fact that God could use you to accomplish his purposes? You might not feel really capable or prepared, but if God could use Jael, he can use you.**

Give each person an index card and a marker.

Say: **I'd like you to think about a way God might use you in your world. I don't want you to predict something that's not true or decide on something now and commit to it. I'd just like you to think about one way God might use you in your life. Be as honest as you can, but remember that you'll be sharing these ideas with other people in the class. When you have your idea, I'd like you to draw a picture of it on the index card. When you have finished, have someone tape the drawing to your back with the picture showing.**

Give students a few minutes to draw their pictures. When they're ready, have students walk around the room and look at one another's drawings. Ask students not to tell one another what their drawings represent. Have students try to guess what each drawing depicts. When students have had a few minutes to guess, ask them to form groups of three and discuss their pictures with the other members of their groups.

After a few minutes, call students together and ask volunteers to explain their pictures. Ask:

~ **When have you had a difficult time understanding God's purpose for your life?**

~ **Is it difficult for you to believe that God could use you to do something amazing and adventurous for him? Explain.**

Say: **God can use you. In fact, he may be using you right now in ways you don't see. It isn't talent or ability that's important. Instead, it's our willingness to let God work through us.**

Worship Time

Say: **God wants to use you to do amazing things for his kingdom. We have to recognize when God is calling us to act, and then we have to be prepared to act. I'd like you to read a Scripture passage and then come up with a series of creative movements to accompany the passage.**

Have students form pairs, and ask pairs to read Jeremiah 29:11. Explain to students that you're going to play some soft instrumental worship music. Give partners time to create a series of creative movements to accompany the passage. They might choose to pantomime the passage to the music, or they might want to do a creative dance to it. As partners are preparing, be available to answer any questions. When partners are ready, play the worship music, and have them make their presentations, one pair at a time.

Closing

Have students remain in pairs.

Say: **God uses the unusual. He calls those people who love him to do amazing things. We don't have to be perfect, just committed. Before we go, I'd like you to take time to commit yourself to God.**

Ask partners to share a few things in their lives that they would like to commit to God in order to be ready to serve him. For example, students might commit to living a more devoted life to God or to giving up a specific sin. After pairs have shared, instruct them to spend time praying for their partners. Close the meeting with a short prayer asking God to use the students to do mighty things.

Age Level Tip

Younger teenagers might have a difficult time approaching this passage from Jael's perspective. Explain to them that they're to read the passage and then think about how Jael might have felt, what she might have been thinking, or what some of her actions might have been that aren't described in the Bible. Then ask groups to write those down in the first person. For example, if students think that Jael might have been nervous, they could write, "I felt really nervous before this whole thing happened."

Employee Profiles

Harry Williams

Experience: Administrator for a large insurance company. Skilled in hiring and supervising people.

Described by former employer as having very strong administrative skills.

Larry Holt

Experience: Former president of a bankrupt computer-manufacturing company. Skilled in supervising large numbers of employees, and knowledgeable in all areas of computer technology. Weak in administration.

Described by former employees as a cheerleader and extremely knowledgeable about the computer industry.

Jessica Henry

Experience: Technical administrator for a large computer company. Extensive knowledge of computers, Internet-related issues, and e-commerce. Weak in supervisory skills.

Described by former employer as a very fast learner but not very helpful in managing employees.

Nicole Morris

Experience: Assistant to the president of a large Internet-related company for five years. Not very knowledgeable about computer-related products but very skilled in hiring and supervising employees. Knows how to get the best out of her employees.

Described by former employer as motivated and administratively strong.

An Odd Weapon

Bible Study

Samson and the Donkey Jaw

Theme

Nothing is impossible with God.

Scripture

Judges 15:9-17; Luke 1:37

Supplies:

You'll need two balloons and two pieces of string per person, newsprint, markers, tape, Bibles, paper, pens or pencils, poster board, slips of paper, a bowl, a timer or a watch with a second hand, and lyrics to the chorus "Ah, Lord God" or another song that reinforces the theme of this study.

Preparation:

Before this session, blow up the balloons, and tie a piece of string to each balloon. Move tables, chairs, and other furnishings to the edges of your meeting area, leaving an open area in the middle of the room.

On a piece of newsprint, write out the list of questions on page 25 of the "Exploring God's Word" section. Post the newsprint where everyone will be able to see it. For the "Worship Time" segment of this study, be ready to share a personal story of a time when God has helped you through a seemingly impossible situation.

Study Judges 15:9-17. Then read the entire session outline. Evaluate all the activities with your group in mind, and make any necessary changes.

Overview

This session teaches students the story of Samson and how he used a donkey jaw to achieve victory over the Philistines. Students will learn that with God their seemingly impossible situations are solvable. Students will

- ∾ experience an impossible situation during a game,
- ∾ learn how God helped Samson out of his impossible situation,
- ∾ explore how God can help them when they're faced with impossible situations,
- ∾ testify about times God has helped them through impossible situations, and
- ∾ pray for each other as they deal with their own situations.

Age Level Tip

If your older teenagers don't enjoy high-action games, try this instead: Tell students you've volunteered the group to clean the church so the regular janitor can have a break. Ask teenagers to form four groups, and assign each group a task such as emptying trash, vacuuming, cleaning the bathrooms, or dusting. Before they begin cleaning, tell them the job has to be done in five minutes. Just as they are set to go and start, let them know you were just kidding.

Ask: • How did you feel when I said your task had to be completed in five minutes?

• What would make it difficult to finish your task in five minutes?

Opener

Say: **Today's study is about Samson and his fight with the Philistines. Let's start with a game that relates to the story.**

Ask one volunteer to play the part of Samson. Tell everyone else they'll play the Philistines. Have the Philistines each tie one balloon to each of their ankles. Say: **Samson, your objective is to pop all of the balloons. Philistines, your objective is to not let your balloons get popped by Samson. If both of your balloons are popped, you're out of the game, and you should sit down out of the way. We'll play the game for five minutes. Go!**

When time is up, count the number of balloons that were popped. Then count the balloons that were not popped. (Unless you have a really aggressive person playing Samson, there should be a greater number of unpopped balloons.)

Say: **That was fun! But Samson's part sure looked difficult, if not impossible.**

Ask:

- ∾ **What made popping the balloons so hard?**
- ∾ **Was it easy or hard to keep your balloons safe? Why?**
- ∾ **Do you think if you had played longer, all of the balloons would have been popped? Why or why not?**

Say: **It seemed pretty impossible to me. Samson was in a similar position with the Philistines. Things looked impossible for him, but God gave him a miraculous victory with the help of a very unusual weapon.**

You may want to share this background information with your students to help them understand the story of Samson and the donkey jaw.

Why were the Philistines ruling over the Israelites? According to Judges 13:1, the Israelites had turned against God, so God had delivered them over to the Philistines for forty years. The Israelites had a bad habit of turning away from God. God would get angry and punish them, and they would repent. This was one of those periods of punishment in the Israelites' history.

Exploring God's Word

Ask students to open their Bibles to Judges 15:9-17. Have a volunteer read the passage aloud.

Have students form three groups. Give each group paper and pens or pencils. Assign one of the following characters to each group: the Philistines, the men of Judah, and Samson. Referring students to the list of questions on the piece of newsprint you posted earlier, ask each group to answer the questions from the perspective of its assigned Bible character and write down its answers.

Write the following questions on newsprint:

~ Why were the Philistines camped in Judah?

~ Why do you think the men of Judah agreed to hand Samson over?

~ Why do you think Samson asked the men of Judah to promise not to kill him?

~ What might have been the response to Samson's captivity? the response of the men of Judah?

~ How did Samson break the ropes?

~ How did you feel as Samson killed one thousand Philistines with the jawbone of a donkey?

Ask each group to share its answers.

Say: **This is a really amazing story. The Philistines, bent on revenge, wanted to capture Samson. And Samson's own people handed him over to the enemy. But instead of giving victory to the Philistines, God gave Samson power, and Samson killed one thousand men with the jawbone of a donkey.**

Have students form new groups of three to four. Instruct each group to create a commercial to sell the donkey jawbone as a weapon. Remind the students that they should use the Bible story to help sell the weapon.

After each group has created a commercial, have groups perform them for one another. Lead everyone in a round of applause for each group.

You may want to share this background information with your students to help them understand the story of Samson and the donkey jaw.

Samson was a Jew who had felt led by God to marry a Philistine woman. Such a marriage wasn't against the law, but Samson's parents were against the union. In Judges 14:4, the Bible explains that the Lord was leading Samson in that direction to create an opportunity for Samson and the Lord to confront the Philistines.

Then ask:

~ **Why do you think God chose to provide Samson with such an unusual weapon?**

~ **What made Samson's situation seem impossible?**

~ **How did God show his power in this situation?**

~ **Did Samson know how God would provide for him? Explain.**

Say: **God made it possible for Samson and the men of Judah to escape a seemingly impossible situation. God provided Samson with a weapon to help him defeat his enemies. And the fact that it was a very blunt instrument magnified God's hand in all of it. God was with Samson and provided him with a victory in this seemingly impossible situation. And he can do the same for you and me.**

Applying God's Word

Ask students to form new groups of two or three. Give each group five slips of paper and a pen or pencil. In their groups, ask participants to discuss situations they face that seem impossible to them. Ask each group to think of five words or short phrases that summarize its discussion. For example, a group might list "parties," "peer pressure," or "saving sex for marriage."

When groups have finished discussing, ask them to share their five words or phrases.

Then say: **The words and phrases in this game describe situations people in this room are facing right now. These are really hard things to be going through. But just like Samson, we do have a way to get through them.**

Ask:

~ **What makes a situation seem impossible?**

~ **How does it feel to face a situation that seems impossible?**

~ **How does it feel to know that God can provide a way through your seemingly impossible situations?**

~ **What are some ways that God helps us through seemingly impossible situations?**

~ **How can we trust God when we're facing these situations?**

Say: **God is with you and will help you if you ask. Luke 1:37 says, "For nothing is** impossible with God." That means anything you face can be overcome if you have God with you! Just as Samson was victorious over the Philistines that day on the hill, we can all be victorious with God in our corner.

Worship Time

Ask everyone to stand. Lead the group in singing the chorus of "Ah, Lord God" or another song that reinforces the theme of this study.

After singing, say: **Let's spend some time sharing personal stories of times God helped us through situations that seemed impossible.**

You may want to begin by sharing your own story. Then encourage teenagers to share their stories with one another. After one or two students have shared, you may want to lead the group in singing the chorus you sang earlier or another song. Continue as long as students are willing to share. Then close the worship time with a prayer of thanksgiving and victory.

Closing

Ask everyone to form pairs and be seated. Direct partners to share with each other ways they can pray for each other. Ask them to discuss seemingly impossible situations they're facing and pray aloud together. Then close by offering the following prayer. Say: **Dear heavenly Father, thank you for your promises to always be with us. Thank you for your provisions as we face our difficulties. Help us seek you when we feel we're facing impossible situations. Help us remember that you'll provide a way through impossibility if we seek you. Thank you for loving us enough to continue to teach us and work with us. Forgive us for all the times we forget to look to you for the answers. In Jesus' name, amen.**

God's Rightful Place

Bible Study
Dagon's Fall

Theme
We must honor God.

Scripture
1 Samuel 4:1–6:20; Proverbs 11:1;
12:16; Romans 5:1; Galatians 2:16;
Colossians 2:13-14; Titus 3:7

Supplies:
You'll need photocopies of the
"Desperate Dialogue" handout (p. 34),
newsprint, tape, Bibles, cardboard, scissors,
colored markers, a trash can, a timer, paper,
and pens or pencils.

Preparation:
Before this session, make a photocopy of the "Desperate Dialogue" handout (p. 34) for
each person. Write the four questions listed in the "Applying God's Word" section (p. 32) on a
piece of newsprint and post it where everyone can see it.

Study 1 Samuel 4:1–6:20. Then read the entire session outline. Evaluate all the activities
with your group in mind, and make any necessary changes.

Overview
This session teaches students about the conflict between the Israelites and the Philistines
and the theft of the ark of the covenant. God's involvement in these events shows that he
wants to be treated with reverence and respect. Students will
- ~ perform a play to depict the incidents described in their assigned verses;
- ~ make and destroy cardboard representations of modern-day idols;
- ~ look for possible causes of modern society's troubles and examine their own behavior

You may want to share this background information with your students to help them understand the story of Dagon's fall.

The Philistines occupied the plains along the east coast of the Mediterranean Sea. The word "Palestine" is derived from the word "Philistine." According to Herbert Lockyer in *All the Miracles of the Bible*, Dagon was "the chief national deity of the Philistines." It had a human-like head, hands, and feet, and the body of a fish. "*Dag* means a 'fish,' and represented the sea from which the Philistines derived so much of their wealth and power...*On*, or *aon*, means 'idol.' "

to determine whether they honor God;

~ participate in a theatrical reading of 1 Samuel 6:1-9 and report, as if they were journalists, what happened in 1 Samuel 6:10-15;

~ understand that Jesus enables us to stand before a holy, sovereign God; and

~ search Proverbs to identify specific ways to honor God.

Opener

Have students form three groups. Assign groups the following verses to act out:

Group 1: Act I—1 Samuel 4:1-3

Group 2: Act II—1 Samuel 4:4-10

Group 3: Act III—1 Samuel 4:11-22

Tell students that the only lines they may speak during the play are the quotes provided in Scripture. Give groups about five minutes to rehearse their parts, and then ask groups to perform the acts in order. After the first group has finished, make sure everyone understands what Scripture events the group was trying to depict.

Then ask:

~ **Why do you think God let the Israelites lose to the Philistines?**

After the second group has finished, make sure everyone understands what Scripture events the group was trying to depict.

Then ask:

~ **Why didn't the presence of the ark of the covenant protect the Israelites?**

After the third group has finished, make sure everyone understands what Scripture events the group was trying to depict.

Then ask:

~ **What did Eli's daughter-in-law mean when she said, "The glory has departed"?**

Say: **Let's take a closer look at this Bible passage.**

Tell Me More

You may want to share this background information with your students to help them understand the story of Dagon's fall.

According to Jenny Roberts, author of *Bible Then & Now*, "The gold-plated wooden chest called the Ark of the Covenant contained the tablets of the law handed down by God to Moses on Mount Sinai. King David took it to Jerusalem and his son Solomon built the Temple to house it." No one is sure what happened to the ark after the destruction of Jerusalem in A.D. 70, although various theories abound.

Exploring God's Word

Have students stay in their groups, and ask someone to read aloud 1 Samuel 5:1-4. Then read aloud the "Tell Me More" box (p. 29) describing the Philistine god Dagon. Give each group some cardboard, scissors, tape, and colored markers. Explain that you want each group to think of some modern-day idols. After several minutes, ask each group to choose an idol to depict using the materials you've supplied.

When groups have finished, display their creations, and have groups explain the idols their creations represent.

Have groups exchange representations, rip them up, and throw them away.

Then ask:

~ **What do these modern-day idols have in common with Dagon?**

~ **How do modern people serve these idols?**

~ **How do you think God feels about modern-day idols?**

~ **Do you think God's feelings are justified? Explain.**

~ **What was it like to rip up the representations you had just created?**

~ **What might it take for you to destroy the power of modern-day idols in your life?**

Ask someone to read aloud 1 Samuel 5:6-12 while you draw three columns on a sheet of newsprint. Be sure everyone can see the newsprint. At the top of the first column, write the words "Philistine Troubles." At the top of the second column, write the words "Modern Society's Troubles." At the top of the third column, write the word "Causes."

Ask students to name the troubles (physical and other) plaguing the Philistines, according to the verses just read, and write these in the first column. Then ask the group to name some troubles (physical and other) that are plaguing modern society, and write these in the second column. Ask students to suggest possible causes for the Philistine troubles, and write their suggestions in the third column. Finally, ask students what might be causing the problems they identified in modern society. Add any of these suggestions to the list in the third column, and circle any suggestions that were also mentioned as causes of the Philistines' troubles.

You may want to share this background information with your students to help them understand the story of Dagon's fall.

In *All the Miracles of the Bible*, Herbert Lockyer points out that the ark symbolized God's power and glory, and clearly showed it was more powerful than Dagon.

Given the importance of the ark, students may question why it has disappeared. You may want to encourage discussion about possible reasons for its disappearance. (For example, students might theorize that it is because the church represents the power and glory of God.)

Ask:

~ **Do these causes of old and new troubles tend to honor or dishonor God? Explain.**

~ **Do you think God causes any of these modern troubles? Explain.**

~ **Who or what do you think is ultimately to blame for modern troubles?**

~ **How would our society and world be different if everyone honored God?**

Give each person a photocopy of the "Desperate Dialogue" handout, and have students form two groups. Have the groups stand on opposite sides of the room, facing each other. Explain that one group will be the Philistines and the other group will be the Priests and Diviners. Ask groups to wait until you've read the opening narration and then respond by reading aloud their parts of the dialogue.

After students have finished reading the "Desperate Dialogue" handout, give each group paper and pens or pencils. Have students pretend they're broadcast journalists who witnessed the events. Ask one group to read 1 Samuel 6:10-12 and write a "news bulletin" recapping what happened in those verses. Ask the other group to read 1 Samuel 6:13-15 and write a news bulletin about what happened in its assigned verses. After five minutes, ask a spokesperson from the first group to read the group's bulletin. When that person has finished, have a spokesperson from the second group read the group's bulletin. Finally, read aloud 1 Samuel 6:19-20.

Ask:

~ **How do you think the people of Beth Shemesh celebrated**

Age Level Tip

The idea of the Philistines making gold likenesses of sores may strike students as odd or even humorous. If older teenagers want to talk about this, encourage discussion about possible reasons for such an outlandish "gift." Focus on the Philistines' motive rather than their methods.

the return of the ark?

~ Why do you think God was so offended by the men who looked into the ark?

~ What does this punishment say about how we should "treat" God?

~ What is the answer to the question "Who can stand in the presence of the Lord, this holy God?"

Say: **We must honor God. God wants our respect, worship, and honor. And God deserves such reverence from us. Let's think about how we can honor God.**

Applying God's Word

Have students form pairs. Instruct partners to take turns answering the questions you've posted on a sheet of newsprint. The questions appear below. To make sure everyone gets the same amount of time, set a timer to go off every two minutes, signaling listeners to become talkers each time the timer goes off.

~ **Have you ever acquired something that caused you trouble? Explain.**

~ **When you acquired it, did your behavior tend to honor or dishonor God? Explain.**

~ **How could you use that thing to honor God?**

~ **What are some ways we can honor God in daily life?**

After sixteen minutes (two minutes per person for each question), ask pairs to wrap up their discussions.

Worship Time

Be sure each person has a Bible. Explain that you're going to repeat the question asked by the men of Beth Shemesh, and each time you do, you want students to silently read the verses you will tell them to read.

Say: **"Who can stand in the presence of the Lord, this holy God?" Read Romans 5:1.**

After several minutes, say: **"Who can stand in the presence of the Lord, this holy God?" Read Colossians 2:13-14.**

After several minutes, say: **"Who can stand in the presence of the Lord, this holy God?" Read Galatians 2:16.**

After several minutes, say: **"Who can stand in the presence of the Lord, this holy God?" Read Titus 3:7.**

After several minutes, ask students to bow their heads in prayer. Say: **Heavenly Father, thank you for being the sovereign Lord. Thank you for being a holy God. Thank you for giving us your Son, Jesus, who makes us able to stand in your presence. Enable us to honor you as we should. In Jesus' name, amen.**

You may want to share this background information with your students to help them understand the story of Dagon's fall.

The behavior of the cows that pulled the cart was miraculous because they didn't act instinctively. By nature, most cows would have turned back to their bawling calves. You may want to lead students to this realization by asking what they would expect the cows to do in such a situation.

Closing

Have students form four groups, and give each group a piece of paper and a pen or pencil. Ask students to look through the book of Proverbs for clues about specific ways to honor God. Challenge students to be specific as they write down several ideas. For example, Proverbs 11:1 says, "The Lord abhors dishonest scales, but accurate weights are his delight." A group could use this proverb to come up with the suggestion "Be honest." Similarly, Proverbs 12:16 says, "A fool shows his annoyance at once, but a prudent man overlooks an insult." A group could use this proverb to come up with the suggestion "Ignore insults." Give students three minutes to think of as many suggestions as possible. Then have groups take turns sharing their findings.

Say: **These are great ideas for honoring God. Remember, God deserves our honor and reverence. Let's try to incorporate these ideas into our everyday lives.**

Desperate Dialogue

(adapted from 1 Samuel 6:1-9)

Narrator:
When the ark of the Lord had been in Philistine territory seven months, the Philistines called for the priests and the diviners and said,

Philistines:
"What shall we do with the ark of the Lord? Tell us how we should send it back to its place."

Priests and Diviners:
"If you return to the ark of the god of Israel, do not send it away empty, but by all means send a guilt offering to him. Then you will be healed, and you will know why his hand has not been lifted from you."

Philistines:
"What guilt offering should we send to him?"

Priests and Diviners:
"Five gold tumors and five gold rats, according to the number of the Philistine rulers, because the same plague has struck both you and your rulers. Make models of the tumors and of the rats that are destroying the country, and pay honor to Israel's god. Perhaps he will lift his hand from you and your gods and your land…
"Now then, get a new cart ready, with two cows that have calved and have never been yoked. Hitch the cows to the cart, but take their calves away and pen them up. Take the ark of the Lord and put it on the cart, and in a chest beside it put the gold objects you are sending back to him as a guilt offering. Send it on its way, but keep watching it."

Unbelievable Power

Bible Study
Elisha and the Bears

Theme
God has amazing power.

Scripture
2 Kings 2:23-25; Exodus 15:6-8

Supplies:
You'll need a description from the "Unbelievable Story Starters" handout (p. 41) for each group of four; three photocopies of the "Tell Me More" boxes on pages 37, 39, and 40; paper; pens or pencils; Bibles; and markers.

Preparation:
Before this session, make enough photocopies of the "Unbelievable Story Starters" handout (p. 41) for each group of four people to have one description from the handout. Make three photocopies of the "Tell Me More" boxes on pages 37, 39, and 40.

Study 2 Kings 2:23-25. Then read the entire session outline. Evaluate all the activities with your group in mind, and make any necessary changes.

Overview
This session teaches students about God's power. They'll get a strong sense of how God uses his power, even in circumstances that seem unbelievable or unfair. Students will
- ~ realize that they can rely on God's power,
- ~ discuss what God's power is like,

~ discover God's power in the life of Elisha,

~ listen to stories about God's power from other parts of the Bible, and

~ reveal areas in their lives in which they need God's power.

Opener

Have students form groups of four. Say: **Have you ever heard a story you knew couldn't be true, but it was told so well that you felt it had to be true? Today I'd like you to create such a story. I'm going to give you a card with a story starter on it. I'd like you to work with your group to create a story based on the story starter, write it down, and then tell us the story as if it really happened. However, I don't want you to devise a way to protect the people being bothered in the story. For example, if your story idea involves an impending attack by wild pigs, please write about how the pigs begin their attack, and write a little of the story, but don't write an ending.**

Assign each group a story starter from the "Unbelievable Story Starters" handout, paper, and pen or pencil. It's OK if more than one group has the same story starter. Give groups several minutes to create their stories. When they have finished writing, have groups trade their stories.

Say: **Here's your chance to have some fun with another group's story. I'd like you to read the other group's story, then write the ending. As you write the ending, please include a way that the people being bothered were protected from their antagonist. So, for example, if your story was about a group of people being attacked by a pack of wild pigs, you might write that the people were rescued by packs of angry, human-defending roaches. Make sure you give enough details so others can understand the story.**

Age Level Tip

You might want to have a group of older teenagers relate an unbelievable story about God's power to the entire group. If you choose to do this, help students by asking them to think of a story they may have heard on the news, perhaps after a natural disaster or another calamity.

Give groups a few minutes to write the endings to the stories of other groups. When they have finished, ask groups to present their stories one at a time. After each group presents, ask:

~ **How believable was this story? Explain.**

~ **What would you add to the story to make it more believable?**

After all the groups have presented, ask:

~ **Which story was your favorite?**

~ **When have you seen God demonstrate his power in a situation that seemed unbelievable?**

~ **How does God use his power?**

Say: **Today we're going to look at an unusual moment in the life of one of God's prophets. This person had an amazing encounter with an unbelievable ending. And in the midst of the event, God demonstrated his power.**

Exploring God's Word

Say: **Let's pretend that a church across town has had trouble recruiting enough Sunday school teachers. The church has asked us to teach three of its Sunday school classes and has assigned us the passage 2 Kings 2:23-25. I'd like you to form three groups and come up with a two-minute lesson that will help your class understand this passage.**

After students have formed three groups, assign one group to teach the children, another to teach the youth, and the third to teach the adults. Hand out copies of the "Tell Me More" boxes to give groups a deeper understanding of the passage.

Give groups five minutes to prepare their lessons. When they're ready, have groups present their lessons, beginning with the group assigned to teach the children. When all groups have presented, have students form new groups of two or three, with one student from each teaching group in each trio. Have groups discuss the following questions.

Ask:

~ **What did you learn about this passage from what you taught?**

~ **What did you learn about this passage from being taught?**

~ **What's the meaning of this story?**

Say: **I'm glad you had a chance to experience this story. But maybe there's more going on here than what we've learned so far. To gain a deeper understanding of a situation, sometimes it helps to get another person's perspective.**

Have students form groups of four. Ask each group to create a two-minute television news-magazine segment based on what happened to the youths in the Bible story. Before groups begin, assign some groups to present segments in favor of Elisha's actions, and others to present segments that are against what Elisha's actions. Give groups several minutes to

Tell Me More

You may want to share this background information with your students to help them understand the story of Elisha and the bears.

The phrase "Go on up, you bald head" apparently carried a lot of significance in this story. Baldness may have been seen as a sign of weakness in ancient Israel (2 Samuel 14:26), and it may have been connected with lack of vigor. Also, when the kids told Elisha to "go on up," they might have been referring to Elijah, who was taken away from the earth in a chariot. If so, the youths telling Elisha to "go on up" was their cry for him to leave the earth.

Age Level Tip

If you have a group of younger teenagers who like to act, have them present their stories without telling the audience what they're presenting. When they have finished, have the audience guess what stories they presented. If you choose to do this, make sure groups have one of their actors present a wrap-up statement at the end so the audience fully understands why the group chose to present that particular situation.

prepare, answering any questions students have.

When groups are ready, have them present their segments. Have one group that favors Elisha's actions go first, then follow with a group that doesn't favor Elisha's actions. Alternate types of presentations until all the groups have presented.

Ask:

~ **Why did the bears hurt the kids?**

~ **If you were Elisha, what would you have done?**

~ **Why did God allow the bears to hurt the kids?**

~ **What does this story say about God's power?**

Say: **This story is very interesting. Elisha was minding his own business when a group of kids began ridiculing him. God demonstrated his power in sending the bears. It's hard to understand every facet of this story, but a few things are clear: When the kids made fun of Elisha, they were ridiculing God's prophet and, therefore, ridiculing God. They were expressing their disdain for the Lord's representative. The bear attack demonstrated the awesome power of God and the need for people to respect that power.**

Elisha and these kids weren't the only people in the Bible to experience God's power. Many other stories in the Bible describe God's power. I'd like you to find one and present it to us.

Ask each group to think of Bible stories that demonstrate God's power. Students might think of stories such as the story of Noah and the ark or God's parting of the Red Sea for the Israelites. Ask each group to select a short passage to read then tell how God's power is evident in the passage. If necessary, help students find the specific stories in the Bible. When groups are ready, have them share their stories.

Ask:

~ **What did you discover about God's power from these stories?**

~ **What causes God to show his power?**

~ **What should our reaction be when we experience God's power?**

Say: **God has been showing his power in the lives of people since history began. He uses his power to help people understand who he is.**

Applying God's Word

Say: **God wants us to trust his power. It's something we can rely on. When we're afraid, whatever we're afraid of, God can use his power to protect us.**

Read Exodus 15:6-8 aloud.

You may want to share this background information with your students to help them understand the story of Elisha and the bears.

Elisha's words had an impact far beyond the young people he was talking to. His statement was also a warning to all of Israel. His curse was intended to say to Israel, "If you continue disobeying God, the same thing that's happened to these kids will happen to your nation." This act also describes Elisha's future as a prophet. Those who listened to Elisha would receive God's covenant blessings. Those who didn't would receive God's curse.

The whys and hows of this story aren't easy to understand and might be difficult to grasp. However, it's a clear and vivid illustration of God's power.

Ask:

~ **What does this passage say about God's power?**

~ **How does God use his power to protect us?**

~ **How does God's power help us do his will?**

Give each student a marker and a sheet of paper. Ask students to each think of one fear he or she has and draw a picture of it on the paper. When students have finished, have them place their pictures face up on the floor and sit next to them.

Say: **I'm going to read Exodus 15:6-8 several times. As I'm reading, I'd like you to go to at least three pictures that others in the room have drawn and write a promise of God's power on the back of each one. For example, you might write, "God can use his power to help you with this fear."**

Give students several minutes to write on the backs of three pictures. Encourage students to look at each picture before they write their comments. When everyone has finished, have students gather in the center of the meeting area and read aloud the comments others wrote.

Worship Time

Say: **God's power is available to us. So whenever we face difficulties or fears, God's power is there. We don't have to live in fear of anything. Let's spend a few moments worshipping God and thanking him for his power.**

Read the following prayer one sentence at a time, and ask students to repeat after you in an attitude of prayer.

Say: **Dear God, we need your power.** (Pause.) **Sometimes we need you to part a sea**

Tell Me More

You may want to share this background information with your students to help them understand the story of Elisha and the bears.

Bethel was the royal cult center of the northern kings (1 Kings 12:29; Amos 7:13). When the kids made fun of Elisha, they were expressing more than a personal dislike of him. Their attitude toward Elisha represented Bethel's attitude toward God. The people of Bethel completely disrespected God's message as spoken through the prophet Elisha.

They also disrespected the work of God's prophets. Elijah and Elisha were known to frequent Samaria. The young people may well have thought Elisha was going up to Samaria to continue Elijah's struggle against royal apostasy.

or heal our hearts. (Pause.) **We struggle with trusting your power, and we try to accomplish things through our own strength.** (Pause.) **Help us trust your power.** (Pause.) **Help us trust your protection.** (Pause.) **When we face situations in which we need your power,** (pause) **help us know you're there,** (pause) **ready to demonstrate what you can do.** (Pause.)

In Jesus' name, amen.

Bonus Idea

If you have a smaller class and students who are comfortable praying aloud for one another, you might want to have students do this closing activity individually instead of in pairs.

Closing

Have students form pairs. Have each pair join with another pair and spend time praying for each other to trust God. When groups of four have finished praying, have the pairs split and join with different pairs to pray. Continue until all pairs have prayed together.

Unbelievable Story Starters

A GROUP OF ANGRY BUFFALO WANT TO EAT YOUR FRONT LAWN.

YOU'RE AWAKENED BY A GROUP OF FIRE ANTS DEMANDING HELP
GETTING YOUR REFRIGERATOR DOOR OPEN SO THEY CAN EAT YOUR FOOD.

AS YOU'RE WATCHING A MOVIE WITH YOUR DATE, A PACK OF WILD MONKEYS
INTERRUPTS TO HARASS YOU ABOUT YOUR CHOICE OF ATTIRE FOR THE DATE.

SEVERAL ANNOYED RATS WANT YOU TO GO DOWN TO YOUR BASEMENT
RIGHT NOW AND CLEAN OUT A PLACE FOR THEM TO SLEEP.

Healing Water

Bible Study

Naaman's Baths

Theme

We can trust God.

Scripture

2 Kings 5:1-19; 2 Corinthians 4:16-18

Supplies:

You'll need various art supplies such as paper, poster board, construction paper, markers, old magazines, and glue; sermon resources such as concordances, Bible commentaries, and books of sermon illustrations; index cards; pens or pencils; Bibles; and modeling clay.

Preparation:

Before this session, set out the art supplies and sermon resources where they'll be easily accessible.

Study 2 Kings 5:1-19. Then read the entire session outline. Evaluate all the activities with your group in mind, and make any necessary changes.

Overview

This session teaches students about trusting God to help and heal them, even when his means seem strange or unusual. Students will

~ discover seemingly odd solutions to problems,

~ explore Naaman's response to God's request,

~ share with God their need and desire to trust him more,

~ understand possible reasons for suffering, and

~ create "community expressions" of trust and faith.

Opener

Have students form two groups, and have the groups sit on opposite sides of the room. Give each group five index cards and pens or pencils. Instruct one group to think of big or small problems they might experience in their lives and write one problem on each index card. (For example, they might describe problems such as test anxiety or trouble getting along with siblings.) Instruct the other group to think of common tasks or activities they do every day, such as brush teeth, watch TV, or hang out with friends, as "solutions." Tell them to write one thing on each index card. Don't let other groups know what each is writing.

When the groups have finished, ask each group to choose one representative to come to the front of the room. Say: **Now we're going to hear about some problems people might have and ways to solve them.** Have the representative from the group that wrote problems on its cards read one problem, and then have the representative from the other group read one "solution." Continue in this manner until all the problems and solutions have been read.

Then ask:

~ **What solutions to some of these problems have you tried? Did your own solutions work? Why or why not?**

~ **What did you think of the group's solutions to the problems? Do you think they would work?**

~ **What would you think if God told you to use one of these solutions to solve a big problem?**

Say: **Today we're going to learn about a man who had a big problem and the seemingly ridiculous solution that God proposed. Let's turn to the Bible to learn about Naaman.**

Exploring God's Word

Have students form three groups, and give each group a Bible.

Say: **Today I'm here as a producer for the TV show "Dateline B.C." I'll be interviewing people for a story about a miraculous event in the life of Naaman, the commander of Aram's army. Your job is to read the story in the Bible and be**

Age Level Tip

Add some drama to make sure younger teenagers truly grasp the story. Have students form five different groups. Assign each group to a character in the story: servant girl, Naaman, king of Israel, Elisha, and Elisha's messenger. Have them act out the event as you read it aloud, with each person playing the role you've assigned to his or her group. After you've read the passage and the students have dramatized it, move on to the interviews.

ready to answer my questions from the perspective of the character or characters you're assigned.

Assign one of the following characters or character groups to each group: the people in Naaman's household, the king of Israel, and Elisha. Have groups read 2 Kings 5:1-19 and talk about what their characters might say about the miraculous event. Then interview the groups with questions such as these:

Ask the people in Naaman's household:

~ **Tell me about Naaman. What kind of man is he?**

~ **I understand that Naaman suffered from a disease. Tell me about it.**

~ **What did you tell Naaman to do about his disease?**

~ **What did Naaman do?**

Ask the king of Israel:

~ **I understand Naaman came to you with an unusual request. Tell me about it.**

~ **How did you respond to Naaman's request? Why?**

Ask Elisha:

~ **What did you do when you heard about the king's response? Why?**

~ **What did you tell Naaman to do? Explain.**

~ **What was Naaman's response?**

~ **What happened next?**

Ask everyone:

~ **How would you have responded if you were Naaman?**

~ **Why do you think God healed Naaman in this way?**

Ask students to shed their character roles and discuss these questions:

~ **What do you think this event tells us about God?**

~ **What do Naaman's responses tell us about ourselves and our relationships with God?**

Say: **It's hard to imagine the situation Naaman found himself in. He suffered from a horrible disease, and he was desperate for help. When God asked him to do something simple and ordinary, he had a hard time trusting. But in the end, he chose to trust God.**

Bonus Idea

As much as possible, play the characters off one another. If the people of Naaman's household respond by saying something about Elisha, for example, turn to the Elisha group for its response. Use the questions provided here to give direction, but don't be afraid to ad lib and build on students' responses. This will help teenagers feel as if they truly are a part of the story.

You may want to share this background information with your students to help them understand the story of Naaman.

Naaman wanted to take home dirt from Israel because he believed Israel to be "holy ground" due to what had happened to him there. He probably intended to spread the soil over a plot of land at his home and have this plot of land serve as a "special place to worship the Lord."

Applying God's Word

Say: **Naaman had a choice in this situation—the choice between faith and disbelief. He had to decide whether to trust God and God's messenger Elisha by following such strange instructions. I'd like each of you to take a few moments to think about your own faith. What situation do you face in your own life that needs God's help and healing? When is it easier to trust God? Would you have trusted God if you were faced with a difficult situation like Naaman's? How can you trust God more?**

Give each person a small piece of modeling clay, and say: **Now you're going to create your own "prayer sculpture." Use this modeling clay to create a sculpture symbolizing either the situation you need God's help with or your feelings about trusting God. Create any symbol you'd like to express what you want to share with God about your situation.**

When students have finished their sculptures, have them each choose a partner. Encourage partners to share with each other as much about their prayer sculptures as they feel comfortable sharing.

Worship Time

Give each student a Bible, and have students turn to 2 Corinthians 4:16-18. Tell students that they're going to complete a responsive prayer in which you'll say a statement and they'll respond by reading one verse of the passage at a time.

Say: **Lord, like Naaman, we suffer, both outwardly and inwardly from afflictions. Can you help and heal us?**

Have students respond by reading 2 Corinthians 4:16 aloud.

Say: **Lord, we don't always understand why difficult things happen to us. Can you help us understand?**

Have students respond by reading 2 Corinthians 4:17 aloud.

Bonus Idea

You may want to create a prayerful mood by playing soft, reflective music as students create their sculptures.

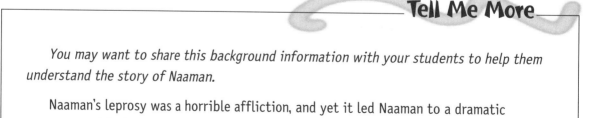

You may want to share this background information with your students to help them understand the story of Naaman.

Naaman's healing happened in this particular way for several reasons. First, God wanted Naaman's healing to be a public matter so others would see and believe in God. Second, Elisha remained inside and instead sent his messenger to Naaman to show that neither wealth nor position could buy healing. Finally, Naaman's healing demonstrated that if we're faithful to God in very small things, God will trust us with more. Naaman was faithful to God's request to do something normal and ordinary, and God in return was faithful in healing Naaman.

Say: **Lord, we want to trust you in all areas of our lives. Can you help us?**

Have students respond by reading 2 Corinthians 4:18 aloud.

Say: **Lord, thank you for your perfect plans for our lives. Please help us trust you with everything—the good things and the not-so-good things. In Jesus' name, amen.**

Closing

Have students return to their groups from the "Understanding God's Word" activity. Point out the art supplies and sermon resources you set out before the session. Explain that you'd like each group to create a community expression of trust in God. For example, groups might create posters or collages using the provided art supplies; they might create "freeze frame" montages using pantomimes or short skits; they might write short stories, poems, or songs; or they might create short "sermons" about trusting God using Scriptures and stories they've

You may want to share this background information with your students to help them understand the story of Naaman.

Naaman's leprosy was a horrible affliction, and yet it led Naaman to a dramatic encounter with the power of God. We don't always understand the reasons God allows his people to suffer, but we can trust that God's plans are perfect.

found in the provided resources. Ask groups to be sure to include details from Naaman's story as well as their own stories and ideas.

When small groups have finished, have them share their creations with the whole group.

Amazing God

Bible Study
Ezekiel's Vision

Theme
God's glory is beyond our comprehension.

Scripture
Ezekiel 1:1-28; Isaiah 6:1-3

Supplies:
You'll need photocopies of the "Ezekiel's Case Study" handout (p. 55), Bibles, pens, colorful markers, newsprint, paper, musical accompaniment for "The Battle Hymn of the Republic" (optional), and tape.

Preparation:
Before this session, make a photocopy of the "Ezekiel's Case Study" handout (p. 55) for each person.

Study Ezekiel 1:1-28. Then read the entire session outline. Evaluate all the activities with your group in mind, and make any necessary changes.

Overview
This session teaches students about Ezekiel's amazing vision and reminds students that God reveals his glory to people. Students will
- ~ compare visions to dreams,
- ~ explore the meaning of Ezekiel's vision,
- ~ draw pictures of Ezekiel's vision,
- ~ evaluate Ezekiel's response to the vision,

~ sings songs declaring God's glory, and

~ thank God for revealing his glory.

Opener

Have students form groups of three. Have each person tell the rest of the trio about the most recent dream he or she remembers. Then have each person tell the rest of the trio about the most memorable or amazing dream he or she has ever had. Encourage students to tell about their dreams in detail, including as much information as possible.

Allow five to ten minutes for trios to discuss their dreams. Then have trios answer the following questions. After each question, ask volunteers to share the trios' answers with the rest of the class.

Ask:

~ **What are dreams?**

~ **Why are some dreams so realistic, while others are just a mixture of disconnected people and events?**

~ **What do you think is the difference between a dream and a vision?**

~ **Many people in the Bible had visions from God; why do you think God would send people visions?**

Say: **In today's session, we'll look at an amazing vision God sent to a man named Ezekiel. As you hear about the vision, think about why God may have sent this particular vision to this particular man.**

Age Level Tip

Older teenagers may want to delve into whether God still speaks to people through dreams, and they may want to relate some examples from their own dreams. This is fine—just be sure to keep the discussion focused on God and his revelations, rather than simply allowing teenagers to talk about their dreams. (This might also be a good time to explain your church's teaching on the subject.)

Exploring God's Word

Have students form groups of four or five. Explain that they are going to play the role of psychiatrists who must help a man decide what his strange dream means. Students will take turns playing the role of the patient, and each group will act as a psychiatric panel.

Begin by giving a little background information about Ezekiel.

Say: **Thank you, doctors, for joining me today. I have a very interesting case study for you. Our patient today is a male, age thirty, named Ezekiel. My assistant will be handing out Ezekiel's patient profiles at this time.** Choose a volunteer to distribute a copy of the "Ezekiel's Case Study" handout to each student. Also distribute Bibles, pens, colorful markers, and several sheets of newsprint to each group. When each group has all its supplies, continue.

Say: **As you can see, the case study has space for you to take notes and jot down questions during the interview. Let's begin.** Choose a student to play the role of Ezekiel,

Tell Me More

You may want to share this background information with your students to help them understand the story of Ezekiel's vision.

Many Bible scholars believe that Ezekiel's vision was ultimately intended to bring hope to the exiled people of Israel. The worst had already happened—the people of Israel had lost their homeland and had been taken captive by a foreign people. But as he related the vision, Ezekiel conveyed the impression that God had arrived to be with his people in Babylon.

and have him or her stand in front of the class. Have that student read aloud Ezekiel 1:1-9 as the other students follow along in their Bibles. Then have "Ezekiel" rejoin his or her group, and have groups answer the following questions. After each question, invite volunteers to share their insights with the rest of the class.

Ask:

~ **What do you think of Ezekiel's vision so far?**

~ **What is the most amazing part of the vision to you?**

~ **What do you think the four living creatures represent?**

~ **How do you think Ezekiel felt when he saw this vision?**

~ **Where did this vision come from? How do you know?**

Say: **Ezekiel must have been amazed at the vision he saw. But he knew the vision came from God. On your case study, write one or two questions you'd like to ask our patient if you could.** Give students several minutes to write. Then have group members read their questions to one another. Invite volunteers to share their questions with the rest of the class.

Say: **To get a more accurate understanding of what Ezekiel saw that day, I want each group to draw a picture of what its members think the vision looked like. I'll give you about five minutes to draw. Remember to refer to your Bibles often as you draw.**

Give groups about five minutes to draw. Then have each group display its drawing for the rest of the class. After each group has presented its drawing, say: **Ezekiel obviously saw this vision in great detail. But that's not all he saw. Let's continue.**

Choose a new Ezekiel to come forward and to read aloud Ezekiel 1:10-14 as the other students follow along in their Bibles. Then have Ezekiel rejoin his or her group, and have groups answer the following questions. After each question, invite volunteers to share their insights with the rest of the class.

Ask:

~ **What's your favorite part of *this* portion of the vision? Why?**

~ Why do you think each living creature had four faces?

~ What do you think the four faces mean?

~ Why do you think fire and lightning are featured so prominently in this vision?

Say: **On your case study, write one or two sentences that you think Ezekiel might have used to describe his vision.** Pause as students write. **Now read your sentences to your group.** After group members have shared, invite volunteers to read their sentences to the rest of the class. Then have each group draw a picture of this part of the vision. Group members can either draw a completely new picture or add to the picture they drew earlier.

Give groups about five minutes to draw. Then have groups present and explain their pictures to the rest of the class. After each group has presented, say: **Ezekiel's vision is getting more and more interesting! Let's see what else it contained.**

Choose a new Ezekiel to come forward and to read aloud Ezekiel 1:15-21 as the other students follow along in their Bibles. Then have Ezekiel rejoin his or her group, and have groups answer the following questions. After each question, invite volunteers to share their insights with the rest of the class.

Ask:

~ What do you suppose the significance of the wheels is?

~ Why did the wheels interlock?

~ What do you think this vision means?

~ Do you think Ezekiel knew what the vision meant? Explain.

Say: **On your case study, write one sentence you think Ezekiel might have used to describe the meaning of this vision.** Give students several minutes to write. Then have group members read their sentences aloud to each other. After groups have shared, invite several volunteers to read their sentences to the rest of the class. Next, have each group draw

Tell Me More

You may want to share this background information with your students to help them understand the story of Ezekiel's vision.

Although Ezekiel's vision may seem difficult to interpret, one theme emerges: God is mighty and marvelous. Some Bible scholars say that the vision was meant to grab Ezekiel's attention (and ours!) and to impart the fact that all of creation—even the parts we've never seen before—is under God's mighty hand. When one realizes that God was showing Ezekiel glimpses into the heavenly realm, it shouldn't be surprising that we, as humans, are awe-struck and confused by what is revealed.

a picture depicting what this part of the vision may have looked like. Again, groups can create new pictures or add on to their existing pictures.

After groups have finished drawing, have them present their pictures to the rest of the class. Then say: **Ezekiel's vision was incredible so far—but there's more to come!** Chose a new Ezekiel to come forward and read aloud Ezekiel 1:22-24 as class members follow along in their Bibles. Then have Ezekiel rejoin his or her group, and have groups answer the following questions. After each question, invite volunteers to share their insights with the rest of the class.

Ask:

~ **What do you think the expanse represents?**

~ **How could the roar of the creature's wings sound like the voice of the Almighty?**

Say: **Ezekiel's vision is almost over. On your case study, write a diagnosis of Ezekiel based on the vision so far.** Give students a few minutes to write. Then have group members read their diagnoses aloud to one another. If you wish, invite volunteers to share their diagnoses with the rest of the class. Then have each group draw a picture of this portion of the vision.

Say: **So far, Ezekiel has seen fire and lightning and four living creatures with four faces each. The creatures have wings, wheels, and more fire and lightning. Pretty incredible! Now we've come to the end of the vision, and it gives us clues to what it all means.**

Choose a new Ezekiel to come forward and read aloud Ezekiel 1:25-28 as students follow along in their Bibles. Then have groups discuss the following questions. After each question, ask groups to share their answers with the rest of the class.

Ask:

~ *Now* **what do you think the vision means?**

~ **Whose voice was speaking in this part of the vision?**

~ **How do you think Ezekiel felt when he realized who was speaking to him in the vision?**

Tell Me More

You may want to share this background information with your students to help them understand the story of Ezekiel's vision.

Ezekiel was a thirty-year-old priest, writing to the Israelites living in exile in Babylon. Babylon was a significant world power at the time and had defeated Judah and taken the people back to Babylon as hostages.

~ **What did Ezekiel do when he realized that he was seeing and hearing "the likeness of the glory of the Lord"?**

~ **What would you do if you had a vision like this one?**

Say: **As you can see, Ezekiel wasn't crazy after all! His vision may seem bizarre to us—it may even have seemed bizarre to *him* at first. But by the end of the vision, Ezekiel had a vivid image of the glory of God. On the bottom of your case study, write in your own words how you would describe the glory of the Lord.**

Give students a few minutes to write. Then have group members read their descriptions aloud. Invite volunteers to share their descriptions with the rest of the class.

Say: **At first we may not be able to really understand Ezekiel's vision or why it was so strange. But when you think about it, it makes sense that we can't envision God's glory in terms of our everyday sights and sounds. The glory of God is so amazing and awesome, it makes sense that it doesn't fit inside our normal images. Let's discuss that a little more.**

Applying God's Word

Have students remain in their groups to answer the following questions. If you choose, have groups share their answers with the rest of the class.

Ask:

~ **Have you ever had an amazing encounter with God? What happened?**

~ **In your estimation, what is the most amazing thing about God?**

~ **How does God reveal himself to you?**

~ **When are you most aware of God's glory?**

Give each group paper and pens. Tell groups that you want them to compose new words to "The Battle Hymn of the Republic." The first sentence and chorus may remain the same. In

Tell Me More

You may want to share this background information with your students to help them understand the story of Ezekiel's vision.

Some Bible scholars believe the winged creatures mentioned in Ezekiel's vision were cherubim. A cherub is a winged, angelic being who exists primarily to glorify God.

their new versions of the song, have groups declare what they think about God's glory and how it applies to their lives. Tell groups they'll have about five minutes to compose their songs.

Circulate among students offering encouragement and help as needed. If groups have trouble getting started, suggest they write about what their eyes have seen and their ears have heard that shows God's glory. For example, roaring thunder, spectacular sunsets, and raging seas all point to God's glory and majesty. Then encourage students to think of how God reveals himself in their lives—how he answers prayer, how he intercedes for them, and how he heals and comforts.

After about five minutes, have each group sing or read its new version of the song. (If you have an instrumental version of "The Battle Hymn of the Republic," play it as an accompaniment for your singers.) Be sure to applaud each group's performance. Then say: **Let's take time right now, right here, to thank God for his glory.**

Worship Time

In their groups, have students read aloud Isaiah 6:1-3. Then have students sit in a large circle on the floor. Explain that as part of a group prayer, each person in the circle will describe a time he or she can praise God for his glory. Then the whole group will respond by saying, "Holy, holy, holy is the Lord Almighty; the whole earth is full of his glory."

For example, a student might say, "When I see lightning and thunder, I think…" and the whole group will respond. Or another student might say, "When I feel alone, I'll remember to say…" and the class will respond. Go around the circle until everyone has had a chance to lead the group in the responsive prayer. Then close by thanking God for his glory that he shows in both big and little ways every day.

Closing

Have students return to their original groups, and give each group a roll of tape. One by one, let groups come to a specified wall of your meeting area and tape their pictures of Ezekiel's vision to the wall. When all the pictures have been taped to the wall, ask:

~ **How are these pictures similar? How are they different?**

~ **How is that like the ways God reveals his glory to all people? to individual people?**

~ **How can you remember to acknowledge God's glory every day this week?**

Close in prayer, praising God not only for his glory, but also for revealing that glory to us.

EZEKIEL'S CASE STUDY

Name: Ezekiel

Sex: Male

Age: 30

Occupation: Priest

Reason for Visit: Vivid Visions

NOTES:_____

_____

_____

_____

_____

_____

_____

_____

_____

_____

Dead Bones Rise

Bible Study

The Valley of Dry Bones

Theme

God alone brings us life.

Scripture

Ezekiel 37:1-14; Acts 1:8a;
Romans 6:4, 7, 11, 19; 8:5b, 16;
2 Corinthians 5:17; John 10:10b

Supplies:

You'll need photocopies of the "Bones in Valley Come Back to Life!" handout (p. 62), photocopies of the bone pattern (p. 61), a live animal, a fake animal (of the same kind if possible), newsprint, tape, markers, Bibles, pens or pencils, and twelve-inch balloons.

Preparation:

Before this session, make a photocopy of the "Bones in Valley Come Back to Life!" hand-out (p. 62) for each person and a photocopy of the bone pattern (p. 61) for each person. Make arrangements to bring a live animal to the session (get a cage, arrange transportation, and so on). Post two sheets of newsprint on a wall in your meeting area.

Study Ezekiel 37:1-14. Then read the entire session outline. Evaluate all the activities with your group in mind, and make any necessary changes.

Overview

This session teaches students how to develop an even deeper and riskier spiritual life through God's Spirit. Students will

~ compare physical life with spiritual life,

~ explore ways God provides his people with new life and gives them his Spirit so they can live this life to the full,

  ~ realize specific ways God's Spirit brings them life to the full,

  ~ affirm ways they see the new life of Christ lived out to the full in one another, and

  ~ commit to do one thing to more fully live out Christ's new life in them.

Opener

Display both the live animal and the fake animal. Point out that one of the animals is "dead" (fake) and the other is alive.

Have two volunteers step up to the sheets of newsprint posted on the wall in your meeting area. Challenge the class to describe qualities and characteristics of each animal that could be explained to someone who is just learning the concepts of "alive" and "dead" (such as an alien from outer space).

As people call out ideas, have one volunteer list all the qualities and characteristics of the living animal on one piece of newsprint. Ideas might include "warm," "heartbeat," "breathing,"

Tell Me More

You may want to share this background information with your students to help them understand the story of Ezekiel and the valley of dry bones.

Ezekiel's vision in this passage is what is called an apocalyptic vision. This type of biblical literature was normally composed when its recipients were experiencing oppressive conditions.

Every detail of such visions was never meant to be interpreted; only the major thrust of the vision was meant to be grasped. Certainly the vision was part of the prophetic message of Ezekiel, but the theological emphasis of the vision was on future things. The vision was meant to encourage the Judean exiles who were living in oppressive conditions and had given up hope of being a nation again or of seeing God's covenants fulfilled.

Through this vision, the Lord promised them that they would live again. Israel would be brought back to life physically, as a nation in its own land. Just as the events in the vision would be miraculous, so would be Israel's restoration. Then this "resurrected" or reborn people would know that God is the Lord. He would send his breath upon them from every direction, and they would experience a spiritual renewal. When Israel was restored and became a nation once again, the people would definitely know that the Lord was responsible for this restoration and that he alone was their God.

Bonus Idea

Here's an alternative activity in case it's too difficult to bring a live animal to the opening activity.

In this activity, volunteers will try to maintain a deadpan stare as other students try to get some kind of reaction from them (such as a changed facial expression or another display of emotion). Select several volunteers from the group who claim they are not easily influenced by others. Have these volunteers sit in chairs facing the rest of the group. Let them know the objective in this activity is for the crowd to try to draw out of them a reaction, expression, or emotion. See which volunteer can resist reacting or expressing emotion the longest. Then lead a short discussion.

Ask:
- **How did it feel to try to retain a deadpan expression while everyone was trying to make you react?**
- **What was it like to try to make the volunteers laugh? Why?**
- **How does this activity illustrate the differences between a dead person and an alive person?**

Have two volunteers step up to the sheets of newsprint posted on the wall in your meeting area. Challenge students to describe qualities and characteristics of dead people and alive people that could be explained to someone who is just learning the concepts of "alive" and "dead" (such as an alien from outer space).

As people call out ideas, have one volunteer list all the qualities and characteristics of a living person on one piece of newsprint. Ideas might include "warm," "heartbeat," "breathing," "eating," "talking," and so on. The other volunteer should list on the other piece of newsprint the qualities and characteristics of a dead person. Some ideas might be "cold," "no heartbeat," "still," "no fun," "boring," and so on.

Ask:
- **How are these qualities and characteristics listed on the newsprint also descriptive of spiritual life? spiritual death? Explain.**
- **What brings physical life? spiritual life?**

"leaping," "eating," "having fun," and so on. The other volunteer should list on the other piece of newsprint the qualities and characteristics of the dead animal. Some ideas might be "cold," "no heartbeat," "still," "no fun," "boring," and so on. Allow group members to interact with the live animal and to manipulate the "dead" animal to help them come up with ideas.

Then ask:

~ In summary, how do you know which animal is dead (fake) and which one is alive?

~ How are these qualities and characteristics listed on the newsprint also descriptive of spiritual life? spiritual death? Explain.

~ What brings physical life? spiritual life?

Say: **Today we'll look at an exciting, epic vision God gave to Ezekiel the prophet. In** this vision, the Spirit of God raised to life an entire valley full of dried-up human bones! By studying this event in the Bible, we can get a better understanding of the power and potential of the Holy Spirit in us and his ability to bring us a full, exciting, spiritual life. Let's look at the life God brings us today.

Exploring God's Word

Read Ezekiel 37:1-14 aloud. After you read the account once, have students form groups of five or more. Just for fun, have each of these groups pantomime a slow motion "rising" of dead bones as you read verses 5-8 again for each group in turn.

Distribute the "Bones in Valley Come Back to Life!" handout (p. 62) and pens or pencils. On the handout, have each group write an eyewitness account of what happened in the valley that day.

After five minutes or so, have each group designate a representative to read its account of the miracle.

Then ask:

~ **What thoughts did you have as you read these articles and accounts of God promising his people new life and spiritual renewal?**

~ **Why do you think God gave his people, and gives us, new life and spiritual renewal to live this life to the full?**

~ **How do we experience God's new life? How do we experience spiritual renewal to live our new life to the full?**

Say: **Just as the story of a valley of dry bones coming back to life is pretty amazing, so is God's gift to us of new life and spiritual renewal. Almighty God, who created all that is, wants to give each of us an exciting, adventurous life—a life to be lived to the full!**

Age Level Tip

As an alternative activity for younger teenagers, try playing a version of Red Light/Green Light. The group begins by lying on the ground (if outdoors) or sitting on the floor (if indoors). Call out, "Dead bones rise!" This will be the students' signal to get up and race toward you. When you call out, "Dead bones die!" they will quickly lie or sit down. The last person moving is out.

Applying God's Word

Give each person an uninflated twelve-inch balloon. Challenge students to do whatever they want to have fun with their balloons—except blow air into them. Then after one minute, have students blow several breaths of air into their balloons, and allow them again to come up with fun ideas for their balloons. Give them two minutes to do this.

When time is up, ask:

~ **Which could you find more uses for (and which was more fun): the uninflated balloon or the inflated balloon? Why?**

~ **How does the balloon best fulfill its purpose? Explain.**

~ **How does this activity demonstrate God's purpose for us (to have new life and** to be filled with spiritual renewal through his Spirit)?

Say: **God has an exciting, purpose-filled life for each of us. God loves us very deeply. He doesn't want us to just pass through this life, living for shallow pleasure and meaninglessness. He wants us to live life to the full! He doesn't want us to just wave "hi" to life. He gives us his Spirit so we can grab hold of life, squeeze it, and get out of it every drop of the unlimited joy, dreams, adventure, purpose, and love this new life holds!**

Worship Time

Give each person at least one marker. If necessary, distribute more balloons so that everyone has one. Read each of the verses or summaries below. As you read each one, have students blow two or three breaths into their balloons. This will represent how the breath of God's Spirit helps them live out their new lives in God to the full.

~ **"I have come that they may have life, and have it to the full" (John 10:10b).**

~ **"We were therefore buried with [Jesus] through baptism into death in order that, just as Christ was raised from the dead through the glory of the Father, we too may live a new life" (Romans 6:4).**

~ **We have been freed from sin's power "because anyone who has died has been freed from sin" (Romans 6:7). "In the same way, count yourselves dead to sin but alive to God in Christ Jesus" (Romans 6:11).**

~ **"Just as you used to offer the parts of your body in slavery to impurity and to ever-increasing wickedness, so now offer them in slavery to righteousness leading to holiness" (Romans 6:19).**

~ **"Therefore, if anyone is in Christ, he is a new creation; the old has gone, the new has come!" (2 Corinthians 5:17).**

~ **"But you will receive power when the Holy Spirit comes on you; and you will be my witnesses" (Acts 1:8a).**

~ **"The mind controlled by the Spirit is life and peace" (Romans 8:6). "Those who live in accordance with the Spirit have their minds set on what the Spirit desires" (Romans 8:5b).**

~ **"The Spirit himself testifies with our spirit that we are God's children" (Romans 8:16).**

~ **"The Spirit helps us in our weakness" (Romans 8:26b).**

Add any verses you think will help students better grasp the concept of "living life to the full." Then have students tie off their balloons and use the markers to draw self-portraits and write their names on one-quarter of their balloons.

Then have students write on each person's balloon one way they see Christ's life being lived out to the full in that person. After a few minutes, have students read their balloons.

Ask:

~ **How do you think God's Spirit helps us live out new life in Christ to the full?**

~ **How did you feel as you read the affirmations of others?**

~ **How was blowing breath into the balloons like how God breathes his Spirit into us to help us live out our new lives to the full? Explain.**

~ **What stands out most in your mind from this experience? Why?**

~ **What are some other things we can do to live out Christ's new life to the full?**

Lead group members in a prayer of thanksgiving for Christ's new life in us and for God's Spirit enabling us to experience this new life to the full.

Closing

Give each person a photocopy of the bone pattern below and a pen or pencil. Have each person write on the bone one risky or radical way he or she will commit to being more alive in Christ. For example, students may write, "I will worship God by singing along with praise music and praying for one hour a day for the next two weeks," "I will share my faith with at least two non-Christian friends over the next two weeks," or "I will perform an act of servanthood or kindness for seven people a day for the next seven days." When students have finished, have each person tape the bone on his or her balloon self-portrait.

Then have students pair up to explain what they have written. Have partners pray for each other to be successful and blessed in living out their commitments. Close by praying that each person will live out Christ's life even more through the power of God's Spirit.

Age Level Tip

Try this idea to help older teenagers understand that getting the most out of life requires risk. Play a short clip from the movie *Parenthood* (Universal Studios, 1989, PG-13). In this clip, an elderly woman no one seems to take seriously makes a great point on how to live life to the full. Begin the clip at one hour, forty-nine minutes and forty seconds with the line "I love you." End the clip at one hour, fifty-six minutes and thirty seconds, when Gil hugs his wife.

Ask: • **What stood out to you in what this elderly woman said?**

• **Which is most like your life and how well you live it to the full: the merry-go-round or the roller coaster? Why?**

• **What risks must you take to more fully live out Christ's life in you? Explain.**

Bone Pattern

Bones in Valley Come Back to Life!

Instructions: You're a newspaper reporter who follows the unusual and "unorthodox" prophetic ministry of Ezekiel. He has chosen to speak with you about his story—something about dry bones coming to life! Read Ezekiel 37:1-14, and write an article as if you were an eyewitness to what is described in that passage. In your article, answer these questions: Who was involved? Where? When? What happened? Do you have any idea why this happened? What is your reaction?

A Marriage With a Message

Bible Study

Hosea's Marriage

Theme

God is faithful.

Scripture

Hosea 1; 3; Exodus 6:7; 33:19;
Deuteronomy 7:6-8; 1 Kings 12:25-33;
2 Kings 14:23-29; 15:8-9, 10, 14, 17-18,
23-24, 25, 27-30; Jeremiah 7:23

Supplies:

You'll need one photocopy of the
"Bachelor/Bachelorette Profiles" handout (p.
68); photocopies of the "Message Through
the Names" handout (p. 69); photocopies of
the "Hard but Happy Ending" handout (p.
70); newsprint; tape; Bibles; markers; old
(clean) socks; various art supplies such as
markers, construction paper, scissors, glue, buttons, and yarn; stationery, and pens or pencils.

Preparation:

Before this session, make one photocopy of the "Bachelor/Bachelorette Profiles" handout
(p. 68) and cut apart the profiles. Make photocopies of the "Message Through the Names"
handout (p. 69) for half the group and photocopies of the "Hard but Happy Ending" handout
(p. 70) for half the group. Post two pieces of newsprint on a wall in your meeting area.

Study Hosea 1; 3. Then read the entire session outline. Evaluate all the activities with your
group in mind, and make any necessary changes.

Overview

This session teaches students about Hosea's marriage to an adulterous woman. His marriage
was a message from God to teach both the Israelites and us about God's faithfulness despite our

unfaithfulness.

Students will

~ identify the unfaithfulness of the Israelites by exploring Scripture,

~ examine the warning God gave the Israelites through Hosea's children,

~ compare the unfaithfulness of the Israelites to our unfaithfulness,

~ compare God's faithfulness to the Israelites and his faithfulness to us, and

~ write a love letter to God, expressing thanks for his faithfulness.

Opener

Say: **Today we'll be playing a little "dating game." You'll have the chance to evaluate three eligible bachelors or bachelorettes and choose the person of your dreams. Before looking at your options, share with the person next to you some characteristics of the man or woman of your dreams.**

Give students time to share, then have three volunteers read aloud the profiles from the "Bachelor/Bachelorette Profiles" handout.

After the volunteers have read the profiles, have students vote for their choices by raising their hands.

Ask:

~ **Why did you choose the person you did?**

~ **Who do you think God would choose for you? Why?**

Say: **In the mid-eighth century B.C., God chose a wife for his prophet Hosea. But rather than choosing someone similar to bachelorette number one or number three, God chose someone similar to bachelorette number two. We're going to study this story to see what in the world God was doing.**

Exploring God's Word

Begin by helping students find the book of Hosea in the Bible. Then have students take turns reading Hosea 1 aloud, a verse at a time.

Ask:

~ **So the big question is, why did God have Hosea marry an adulterous wife?**

Then say: **In order to understand why God had Hosea marry an adulterous wife, we have to understand the situation at that time. We're going to draw a picture depicting Hosea's time. The book of 2 Kings gives us details about what was happening in Judah during the time of Hosea. We're going to examine six passages that discuss leaders and how they led their people.**

Choose one person to be the artist, and have that person stand with a marker at one of the pieces of newsprint you posted earlier. Have everyone else form six groups (it's OK if a group consists of one person). Assign each group one of the following Scripture passages.

You may want to share this background information with your students to help them understand the story of Hosea's marriage.

While David was king of Israel (2 Samuel 5:4-5), he made his share of mistakes, but he loved God and eventually did what was right in God's eyes (2 Samuel 11; 22; 24:25). Then his son Solomon became king (1 Kings 2:12). Solomon was wise and rich, but he turned away from the Lord, and therefore his favor ended. When Solomon died, God gave part of Solomon's kingdom to one of his officials (1 Kings 3:7-15; 11:31-40).

Thus there was a northern kingdom (Israel)—ruled by Solomon's official Jeroboam and his heirs—and a southern kingdom (Judah)—ruled by Solomon's son Rehoboam and his heirs. Hosea came to speak to the northern kingdom during its final days.

Instruct each group to read the assigned passage and be ready to tell the artist what the passage reveals.

Jeroboam: 2 Kings 14:23-29

Zechariah: 2 Kings 15:8-9

Shallum: 2 Kings 15:10

Menahem: 2 Kings 15:14, 17-18

Pekahiah: 2 Kings 15:23-24

Pekah: 2 Kings 15:25, 27-30

Give groups a few minutes to read their passages. Then have each group tell the artist what the passage reveals about the circumstances of the time. Have the artist draw pictures or write words that depict what the groups are reporting from Scripture.

When each group has reported, say: **Jeroboam must have been a very evil king since the Bible says all these other kings followed in the evil footsteps of Jeroboam.**

Have a volunteer read 1 Kings 12:25-33 aloud.

Say: **Israel wasn't doing so well! The Israelites were doing everything they weren't supposed to be doing: worshipping false gods, killing their leaders in order to gain power, and so on. Things were crazy. And that's why Hosea came to give the Israelites a message. God knew that they were leading themselves to destruction, but the people just didn't seem to realize it.**

So what was the message Hosea gave them? Did he just tell them, "You'd better change, or else"? No, Hosea had to go through a difficult situation himself to deliver a powerful message to the Israelites. To understand this message, we must understand the symbolism in Hosea's marriage.

You may want to share this background information with your students to help them understand the story of Hosea's marriage.

So why look up Jeroboam, Zechariah, Shallum, Menahem, Pekahiah, and Pekah in the book of 2 Kings? A little cross-referencing and a good study Bible make the answer apparent. First, Hosea 1:1 names many leaders of Judah and one leader of Israel. Since the rest of Hosea deals with Israel, we want to know more about Israel than Judah. We can read the notes in a study Bible to find out when the leaders of Judah were in power, then we can find out which leaders of Israel were in power at those same times.

Ask:

~ **From what you know, who might Hosea and Gomer represent?**

Say: **In this story, Hosea represents God, and Gomer represents the people of Israel. We're going to work in two groups to further understand the message that Hosea was presenting not only through his words, but also through his situation.**

Age Level Tip

Depending on the personality of your group, older teenagers may not enjoy creating puppets and using them for a puppet show. If not, simply instruct students to act out what they learned from their handouts.

Have students form two groups. Give each person in the first group a photocopy of the "Message Through the Names" handout. Give each person in the second group a photocopy of the "Hard But Happy Ending" handout. Give both groups several old socks and various art supplies such as markers, construction paper, scissors, glue, buttons, and yarn.

Instruct groups to complete their handouts, then to use the supplies you provided to create sock puppets that represent the characters in the story. When groups have finished creating their puppets, ask them to use the puppets to perform puppet shows, demonstrating what they learned from their handouts.

Lead a round of applause for each group's puppet show. Then say: **Good job deciphering the symbolism in Hosea's marriage. Now let's take a look at how this story relates to us.**

Applying God's Word

Choose a new volunteer to be the artist. Have that person stand with a marker at the other piece of newsprint you posted earlier.

Say: **Let's work together to create a picture that illustrates our world. What are some quick ways we can describe our country, neighborhoods, and schools today?**

Encourage students to call out ideas for drawings and words that describe their world. As they call out ideas, have the artist draw or write the ideas on the newsprint. Then say: **Now let's**

You may want to share this background information with your students to help them understand the story of Hosea's marriage.

So what was the problem with building high places and burning incense? These actions were "evil," as Scripture says, because they were in a direct defiance of the first two commandments (Deuteronomy 5:6-10). During Hosea's time, the cultic worship of Canaanite gods was heavily influencing the culture in Israel. Many were turning to those false gods instead of the one true God who had chosen them and rescued them many times already.

compare the picture we created of Hosea's world with the picture we created of our world.

Ask:

~ **What similarities do you see?**

~ **What differences do you see?**

~ **Considering the behavior of the people in Hosea's world, what did they deserve from God?**

~ **Considering what we do, what consequences do we deserve from God?**

~ **As God sent Hosea to warn his people, what does God do to warn us of the consequences of our actions?**

~ **How was God faithful to the Israelites?**

~ **How is God faithful to us?**

~ **How should we respond to God's faithfulness?**

Say: **In spite of our unfaithfulness to God—like the unfaithfulness of Hosea's wife—God remains faithful to us. He hasn't given us what we deserve: rejection and destruction. Let's thank God for that faithfulness.**

Worship Time

Give each person a piece of stationery and a pen or pencil, and encourage teenagers to spread out and find their own space in the meeting area. Say: **God is amazingly faithful to us despite our unfaithfulness. Let's spend a couple of minutes writing letters to God, expressing our gratitude. Write about specific incidents when God has been faithful to you.**

Give students several minutes to write their letters.

Closing

Have students form groups of two or three people and share the letters they wrote to God. Ask them to pray with each other, thanking God for his faithfulness.

Bachelor/Bachelorette Profiles

Bachelor/ Bachelorette

This person is your age. This person's job is compatible with yours, and this person will have lots of time to spend with you. This person is intelligent, good-looking, and athletic. This person loves God more than anything. This person is fun and exciting to hang out with and always makes you laugh. This person hasn't dated many people but is loyal to every commitment and knows that you're "the one."

Bachelor/ Bachelorette

This person is attractive and fun. This person has dated many people, sometimes two at a time. This person has a reputation for being overly flirtatious and has never remained committed in any dating relationship.

Bachelor/ Bachelorette

This person is older than you are and is artistically talented. This person doesn't really like school but may one day be a successful musician. This person loves to do romantic things and always makes you feel loved. This person hasn't dated a lot of people but is looking for a soul mate.

Message Through the Names

God gave Hosea and Gomer three children. At that time, people's names held great significance. Hosea and Gomer's children's names were important; they were messages to the Israelites.

The first child's name was _____ (Hosea 1:4).

This name meant "God scatters." It was a prophetic name because Hosea knew that as a result of the Israelites' evil behavior, the Assyrians were going to attack and deport them. History shows that this happened in 724 B.C. Read 2 Kings 17:5-6 to find out what happened to the Israelites.

The second child's name was _____ (Hosea 1:6).

This name expressed a reversal of the love that God had earlier shown the Israelites, but would show them again later. Read Exodus 33:19 and Deuteronomy 7:6-8 to understand the love God had shown them.

The third child's name was _____ (Hosea 1:9).

This name expressed a break in the covenant relationship between God and Israel. Read Exodus 6:7 and Jeremiah 7:23 to understand God's relationship with the Israelites.

The messages God was giving the people through Hosea and Gomer's children were harsh and frightening. With your group, create a puppet show depicting what you learned from this handout. Be sure to include the names of the children, the message each one brought with the name, and what God meant by each message.

The Hard but Happy Ending

God had Hosea marry an unfaithful woman and have children with her. Her unfaithfulness was representative of the Israelites' actions. Hosea's actions were representative of God's actions. Read Hosea 3 to see what happened after his wife bore three children and then had an affair and left him.

The message was that despite Gomer's unfaithfulness (and the Israelites' unfaithfulness), Hosea still showed love to Gomer (and God would still show love to Israel). With your group, create a puppet show that depicts what you learned from this handout. Be sure to show what happened to Hosea and Gomer. Also make the point that their relationship was comparable to the relationship between the Israelites and God.

Sight and Salvation

Bible Study
Jesus Places Spit on a Blind Man

Theme
God makes us whole.

Scripture
Mark 8:22-26; John 9:39

Supplies:
You'll need photocopies of the "Experiencing Blindness" handout (p. 76), scissors, photocopies of the "Eye Exam" handout (p. 77), blindfolds, Bibles, pens or pencils, newsprint, markers, and a children's picture puzzle with about as many pieces as you have students.

Preparation:
Before this session, make enough photocopies of the "Experiencing Blindness" handout (p. 76) for each person to have a card, and cut apart the cards on each handout. Make a photocopy of the "Eye Exam" handout (p. 77) for each person.

Study Mark 8:22-26. Then read the entire session outline. Evaluate all the activities with your group in mind, and make any necessary changes.

Overview
This session is about Jesus' use of his own saliva to heal. This story reminds students that Jesus can heal their spiritual blindness and can use them to bring others to him for hope and healing. Students will

 experience blindness,

~ examine the blind man's story and discuss his "case history,"

~ identify their own blind spots,

~ identify friends and others they might bring to Christ for healing, and

~ see how Jesus makes us whole.

Opener

Have students form pairs, and give each pair a blindfold. Say: **To begin today's study, we're going to experience what it is like to be blind. In your pair, I'd like you to choose one partner to be blind first. The other partner will tie the blindfold on the "blind" partner's head.**

When each pair has one blindfolded partner, give the other partner in each pair one card from the "Experiencing Blindness" handout, and say: **Now I'd like the sighted partner in each pair to read the instructions on the card. Then use the instructions to help your blind partner identify the object on the card.**

Give students a few minutes to identify the objects. Then have partners switch roles so that the sighted partner is now blindfolded. Give each new sighted partner a new card, and have pairs repeat the process.

After students have identified the objects, ask:

~ **How easy was it to identify the objects without using your sense of sight? Explain.**

~ **What would it be like to be blind? What would change the most in your life?**

~ **Have you ever experienced blindness of any sort? Explain.**

Say: **Let's turn to the Bible to discover Jesus' response to one blind man.**

Age Level Tip

Rather than having older teenagers experience blindness in this manner, you might want to have pairs brainstorm different types of blindness (for example, spiritual blindness) and create one poster for each type of blindness they think of. Then have pairs share their posters with the rest of the group.

Exploring God's Word

Have pairs combine to form three groups. Explain that each group will act as a team of doctors. The doctors' task will be to determine what happened in the case of the blind man as described in Mark 8:22-26. Give each group Bibles, photocopies of the "Eye Exam" handout, and pens or pencils. Have groups begin their task by reading the "case history" in the Bible. Then assign each group a different part of the handout.

When groups have finished the handout, give each group newsprint and markers. Say: **Now that you've gathered your information about the patient and his case, I'd like you to prepare a presentation to share your findings with the rest of the group. Use the** newsprint and markers to create visual aids to go along with your presentation. You might create illustrations, charts or graphs, or notes. Make your presentation as interesting and informative as possible. Remember, you will be making your presentation to other teams of doctors.

Bonus Idea

If you have a student who is blind or visually impaired, ask ahead of time if he or she would be willing to share some of his or her experiences with the rest of the class.

When groups have finished preparing, have them share their presentations one at a time. Then ask:

~ **Why do you think Jesus chose to heal the man in this way?**

~ **What does this event tell you about Jesus?**

~ **What does this event tell you about the blind man's friends?**

~ **Do you think you would do this for a friend who was suffering from blindness? Explain.**

~ **Why do you think Jesus took the man out of the village and told him not to return to the village?**

~ **Based on your exams, what do you think Jesus' response is to human blindness?**

Say: **Jesus responds to human blindness (both physical and spiritual) with help, hope, and healing.**

Applying God's Word

Say: **Now you're going to complete your own "I Exam." First, I'd like you to think of blindness you may suffer from in your own life. For example, you may sometimes be blind to the loneliness of unpopular students in your school. Turn over your handout and think about those blind spots. Write them down at the top of your handout.**

Tell Me More

You may want to share this background information with your students to help them understand the story of Jesus' healing of the blind man.

Jesus appeared to fail in healing the man the first time he tried. There are a few possible explanations for this. "First, Jesus heals people in a variety of ways. In this case, he used a two-step process. Second, and more importantly, achieving spiritual insight may be a gradual process rather than a dramatic event. The disciples, like the blind man, had a measure of insight, but still needed the help of Jesus for further understanding" (*Quest Study Bible*, page 1394).

Give students a few minutes to do this, and then say: **For the second part of your "I Exam," I'd like you to remember the blind man's friends in the story. They interceded for him and brought him to Christ so that Christ could heal his blindness. Think of a few friends or others you could bring to Christ for healing and redemption, and write their names on the bottom of the handout.**

Worship Time

Give each student a Bible, a pen or pencil, and a piece of a children's picture puzzle. If you have more puzzle pieces than students, take the remaining pieces yourself. Explain to students that you'd like them to create their own prayers of commitment based on John 9:39. Have them paraphrase the verse using some of the blind spots and people they thought of in the "Applying God's Word" activity. For example, someone might say, "Lord, I know you've come into this world so the blind will see. Please help me to discover my "blind spots," such as my blindness to your great love for me. Help me also to bring my friends Joe and Jane to you so that you can heal their blindness."

Have students write their prayers on their puzzle pieces.

Tell Me More

You may want to share this background information with your students to help them understand the story of Jesus' healing of the blind man.

Why did Jesus choose to use his own saliva to heal the blind man? Surely he could have used his divine powers and not even touched the man. However, it's possible that "Jesus recognized the man's need for increased faith and offered his physical action to raise his expectations. If so, the man's spiritual sight was strengthened as physical sight was imparted to him" (*Quest Study Bible*, page 1394).

Closing

Have students fit their puzzle pieces together to form one puzzle.

Ask:

~ **How is this complete puzzle like your life after Jesus heals you?**

~ **How would your life be different if Jesus completely healed your blindness?**

~ **What would your response be to the gift of healing?**

Say: **Just as we worked together to make this puzzle one perfect whole, Jesus can heal our blindness and make us complete.**

Close in prayer, asking God to heal the blindness of everyone present.

Experiencing Blindness

The object you're trying to get your partner to guess is an apple.
Help your partner discover what the object is by describing its smell.
Don't give your partner any other hints!

The object you're trying to get your partner to guess is a dog.
Help your partner discover what the object is by describing how it feels
to touch a dog. Don't give your partner any other hints!

The object you're trying to get your partner to guess is a raindrop.
Help your partner discover what the object is by describing the way it feels.
Don't give your partner any other hints!

The object you're trying to get your partner to guess is an orchestra.
Help your partner discover what the object is by describing the way it sounds.
Don't give your partner any other hints!

Eye Exam

Patient Background

Share a bit about the patient's background by answering these questions:

- Who is the patient?
- Where did he come from?
- How did he become blind?
- How did he meet Jesus?

Event

Discuss the event that restored the blind man's sight by answering these questions:

- Where did this event occur?
- What did Jesus use to restore the man's sight?
- What effects did this "medicine" have?

Prognosis

Imagine what may happen in the blind man's future by answering these questions:

- Do you think the man will be able to see for the rest of his life? Explain.
- How do you think his life will be different from this point on?

Fallings and Failings

Bible Study
Eutychus' Fatal Nap

Theme
God is full of grace.

Scripture
Acts 20:6-12

Supplies:
You'll need photocopies of the "Find the Mistakes" handout (p. 84), photocopies of the "Flip Puzzle" handout (p. 85), a tarp, a raw egg for each person, permanent markers, colorful markers, tape, Bibles, pens or pencils, scissors, song lyrics, musical accompaniment (optional), and yarn.

Preparation:
Before this session, make a photocopy of the "Find the Mistakes" handout (p. 84) for each pair of students and a photocopy of the "Flip Puzzle" handout (p. 85) for each person. Cut three twelve-inch lengths of yarn for each person.

Study Acts 20:6-12. Then read the entire session outline. Evaluate all the activities with your group in mind, and make any necessary changes.

Overview
This session teaches students about Eutychus and a mistake he made. This Bible study guides youth to explore their feelings when they fail or make mistakes and actions they can take to put their lives back together through grace. Students will

~ experience brokenness and the frustration of trying to fix it,

~ find mistakes in a retelling of the Eutychus event by focusing on key words,

~ identify actions they think doom them to future failure,

~ replace failure with deliberate choices to begin again, and

~ rejoice in the freeing power of God's grace.

Opener

Take students outside, or spread a tarp over the floor in your meeting area. Give each person a raw egg, and make permanent markers and colorful markers available. Instruct students to put their initials on the eggs with permanent markers. Then let students decorate their eggs with colored markers to personalize them.

When students have finished decorating their eggs, say: **Hold your egg straight out from your body, safely in the palm of your hand. On my cue, turn your hand over and let your egg fall. Ready? On your mark, get set, drop.**

Wait for students to drop their eggs, then say: **Now put your egg back together—at least the shell part. Here's some tape to help you.**

When students protest that it's impossible to put the eggs back together, urge them to try anyway. Applaud every small success at getting any piece of an egg back together.

After a few minutes, have youth show the results of their egg reassembly. Say: **It's impossible to put these eggs totally back together again. We might be able to get the shell back together, but the yolk will never go back into the egg. In the same way, once someone has died, you can't bring that person back to life. And some mistakes seem totally unfixable. Let's find out what happened to a young man named Eutychus who fell out of a third-story window and couldn't be put back together.**

Bonus Idea

As an alternative to the activity involving raw eggs, consider this idea: Have students form groups of three. Have trios race to name twenty-five things that can't be put together once they have been dropped or broken. Examples include raw eggs, mirrors, glass, and statues.

Then ask: **What nonmaterial things are hard to put back together once they're broken?** Examples include trust, honor, and reputations.

Say: **In the same way, once someone has died, you can't bring that person back to life. And some mistakes seem totally unfixable. Let's find out what happened to a young man named Eutychus who fell out of a third-story window and couldn't be put back together.**

Exploring God's Word

Have students form pairs. Give each pair a photocopy of the "Find the Mistakes" handout, a Bible, and a pen or pencil. Say: **Correct the mistakes in this bogus retelling of the story of Eutychus so it matches the scriptural story of Eutychus. One partner will read the passage while the other follows on the handout and says "stop" whenever**

You may want to share this background information with your students to help them understand the story of Eutychus.

The name Eutychus means "fortunate." Though his name sounds unusual to us, it was a common name during Bible times. Eutychus was a young person who experienced a miracle. He was one of the few people God raised from death back to life. The way he died was most unusual: Eutychus was sitting in the window listening to Paul preach. Paul preached so long (until midnight and then on until daybreak) that Eutychus was overcome by sleep and fell out of a third-story window to his death. Paul interrupted his preaching just long enough to revive Eutychus. So Eutychus' name took on an even more special meaning. He was not only fortunate but also blessed by God.

something doesn't match. Write in the corrections at each stop.

When students have finished, read aloud the "Find the Mistakes" answer key, pausing before each mistake (in italics) to allow group members to say together the correct information (underlined). Then ask:

~ **Can you relate to Eutychus? In what way?**

~ **What part of his situation is most like yours?**

~ **When have you needed a fresh start?**

~ **If you were Eutychus, would you have wanted to go back to church? Why or why not?**

Say: **Eutychus made a mistake by sitting in the window when he was sleepy. It was an innocent mistake, but it cost him his life. One of the most innocent mistakes we make causes us great pain. This mistake is to assume that, just like our broken**

Find the Mistakes Answer Key

Acts 20:6-12

But we sailed from *Bethlehem* (Philippi) after the Feast of Unleavened Bread, and five days later joined the others at *Nazareth* (Troas), where we stayed seven days. On the *last* (first) day of the week we came together to break bread. *Peter* (Paul) spoke to the people and, because he intended to leave the next day, kept on talking until *one o'clock* (midnight). There were many *lambs* (lamps) in the upstairs room where we were meeting. Seated in a *pew* (window) was a young man named *James* (Eutychus), who was sinking into a deep *worship* (sleep) as Paul talked on and on. When he was *deeply worshipping* (sound asleep), he fell to the ground from the *first* (third) story and was picked up *safely* (dead). Paul went down, threw himself on the young man and *talked sternly to* (put his arms around) him. "Don't be alarmed," he said. "He's *sorry* (alive)!" Then he went upstairs again and broke bread and ate. After talking *no more* (until daylight), he left. The people took the young man home alive and were greatly *angry* (comforted).

You may want to share this background information with your students to help them understand the story of Eutychus.

It was in Troas that Paul met and revived Eutychus. Troas was a city in the Roman province of Asia, located about ten miles from ancient Troy. Its full name was Alexandria Troas, and it served as an important seaport for connections between Macedonia and Greece, and Macedonia and Asia Minor. Paul visited Troas on his second and third missionary journeys.

eggs, we can't be put back together once we've done something wrong.

Ask:

~ **What are some wrongs people think doom them to never being fixed?**

~ **What does this Bible passage say about the assumption that we can't be put back together?**

Say: **Though we can never erase the past and the damage we've done, we can move forward to create new good. Focusing on past mistakes means making more messes. Accessing grace means cleaning up our lives and putting things back together.**

Applying God's Word

Say: **The difference between staying in past messes and choosing a clean start is determined by the moves you make. Let's practice moving forward with these flip puzzles.**

Give each person a photocopy of the "Flip Puzzle" handout, and have scissors available. Show students how to fold the handouts, using the instructions on the flap of the handout. (Many will remember this retro activity from elementary school. Call on older students to help you if you've never done a flip puzzle before.)

Have students form pairs. Challenge pairs to use their flip puzzles to find eight examples of how to choose a fresh start. They begin by inviting their partners to pick an outside word: "grace," "gives," "fresh," or "starts." They then take turns flipping the puzzle, spelling the outside words, then the phrases on the inside, and then opening the flap of the phrase they pick to find out how to start over after making that mistake.

Age Level Tip

Younger teenagers may give examples of unforgivable sins that are very different from those of senior high youth. They may speak about lying while older youth speak about sleeping around. Take seriously (and insist that the group take seriously) whatever examples younger teenagers offer. The fear that we can't approach God after a certain mistake is more critical than the severity of the sin.

You may want to share this background information with your students to help them understand the story of Eutychus.

Eutychus wasn't the only person God raised from death. The Bible records the stories of several others, including the son of the widow of Zarephath, helped by Elijah (1 Kings 17:17-23); the Shunammite's son, helped by Elisha (2 Kings 4:32-37); the young man in Elisha's tomb whose body touched Elisha's bones (2 Kings 13:21); a widow's son, raised by Jesus (Luke 7:11-15); Jairus' daughter, raised by Jesus (Luke 8:49-56); Lazarus, raised by Jesus (John 11:43-44); and Dorcas, helped by Peter (Acts 9:37-42). Hebrews 11:35 tells us that possibly even more Old Testament women received their dead back, raised to life again.

The eighth flap is blank for youth to write another mistake and a way to start fresh after making that mistake. Have them do this after three rounds of the game, urging each person to write a different mistake on his or her puzzle.

After all pairs have tried all eight flips, ask:

~ **How does God's grace help us make fresh starts?**

~ **How does God's grace help us leave past messes in the past?**

~ **What can we do to access God's grace?**

~ **What makes some people believe they must stay on a bad path once they take a step down that path?**

~ **What has been, or could be, your greatest success in accessing God's grace to make a change?**

Say: **God is full of grace, and God's grace can help us make fresh starts. Even though we can never put ourselves back together, God can make us whole again. Let's worship God for his grace.**

Worship Time

Ask students to suggest choruses and songs that remind them of God's grace (for example, "Great Is Thy Faithfulness" or "Thy Word.") Provide lyrics to help in the brainstorming.

Sing a verse from each song as praise for God's grace.

Closing

Give each person three twelve-inch strands of yarn. Instruct

Age Level Tip

Some older teenagers may consider the flip puzzle childish; others will like it because it reminds them of their childhood days. Approach this with a spirit of fun, and your senior highers will enjoy it along with you. If they openly question the activity, explain that as their fingers move, they'll be reminded that their choice of movement affects how well they access God's grace. Suggest that they make their own flip puzzles if they prefer.

youth to braid the yarn into ankle bracelets as reminders of God's grace.

Say: **Each strand of the bracelet is like a fresh start in life. Wear your bracelet at least through the next week to remind yourself to live by grace and to change past mistakes rather than staying tied to them.**

When students have finished their ankle bracelets, close in prayer, thanking God for his grace.

Find the Mistakes

Find the mistakes in this retelling of Acts 20:6-12.

But we sailed from Bethlehem after the Feast of Unleavened Bread, and five days later joined the others at Nazareth, where we stayed seven days. On the last day of the week we came together to break bread. Peter spoke to the people and, because he intended to leave the next day, kept on talking until one o'clock. There were many lambs in the upstairs room where we were meeting. Seated in a pew was a young man named James, who was sinking into a deep worship as Paul talked on and on. When he was deeply worshipping, he fell to the ground from the first story and was picked up safely. Paul went down, threw himself on the young man and talked sternly to him. "Don't be alarmed," he said. "He's sorry!" Then he went upstairs again and broke bread and ate. After talking no more, he left. The people took the young man home alive and were greatly angry.

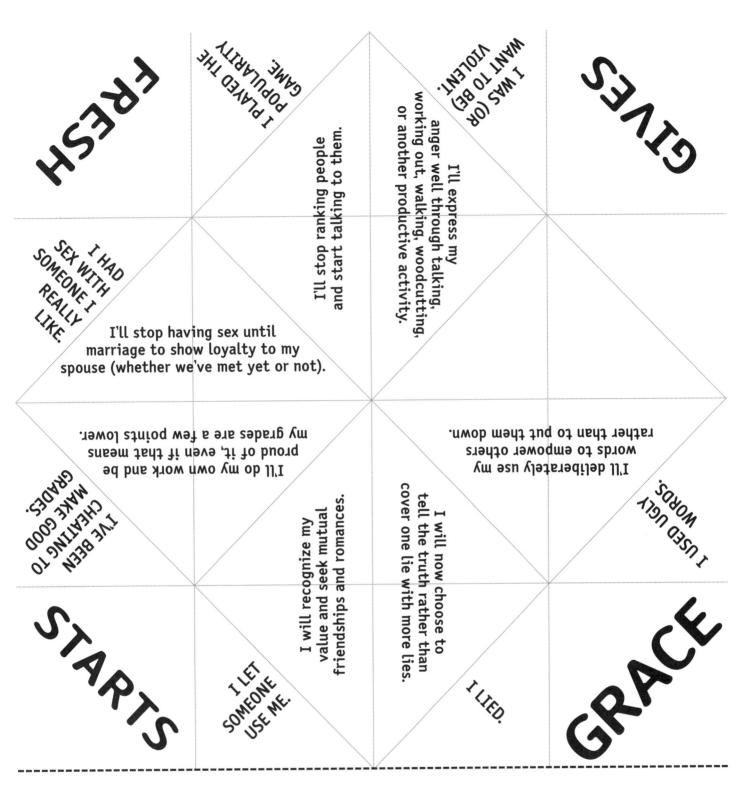

Folding Instructions

1. Cut off this piece with the instructions. What's left is a square piece of paper.

2. Place the paper on a flat surface, printed side down. Fold the four corners so that they meet in the center of the paper. You should see the words "grace," "gives," "fresh," and "starts."

3. Turn the new square over so that the words just noted are face down. Fold the four new corners so that they meet in the middle of the square. The phrases "I

lied," "I let someone use me," "I've been cheating to make good grades," "I had sex with someone I really like," and so on are now visible.

4. Fold this square in half and make a rectangle. "Grace" and "gives" should be visible on one side; "fresh" and "starts" on the other side. Stick your fingers under the flaps, and you're ready to flip the puzzle back and forth to reveal words and open flaps.

Snake Attack

Bible Study
Paul and the Snake

Theme
God protects us.

Scripture
Acts 28:1-6; Psalm 144:1-2

Supplies:
You'll need a blindfold or bathroom tissue for each person, two foam bats or two rolled-up newspapers, Bibles, paper, pens or pencils, items used for protection in some way (such as a helmet, a sword, steel-toed boots, football pads, a small piece of fence or wall, and shaving cream), large pieces of cardboard, markers, masking tape, construction paper, and glue sticks.

Preparation:
Before the session, clear all furniture and other obstacles from the center of the meeting area. Study Acts 28:1-6. Then read the entire session outline. Evaluate all the activities with your group in mind, and make any necessary changes.

Overview
This session teaches students about God's protection of Paul and that God protects us in similar ways. Students will
~ practice protecting themselves or others,
~ explore the way God protected Paul from the bite of a deadly snake,

~ find assurance of God's protection, and

~ identify ways God protects us.

Opener

Blindfold one volunteer either with a handkerchief or by wrapping bathroom tissue around the volunteer's head several times and tying it in the back. Give this blindfolded volunteer either a foam bat for each hand or a rolled-up newspaper for each hand.

Say: **Our volunteer is the snake. The snake will try to "bite" people by touching them** (*not hitting them*) **with the bats which represent fangs. To find the other people, our snake must make a hissing noise. When the snake hisses, everyone else must shout, "Snake!" Everyone must stay in the center of the meeting area. You may not go past the furniture.**

Allow students to play for several minutes. When someone is bitten by the snake, blindfold that person and have him or her join the snake. He or she will stand behind the snake and place one hand on the snake's shoulder, leaving the other hand free to "bite" other students with his or her bare hand. Continue in the same way until everyone has been bitten.

Then ask:

~ **What was your strategy for staying away from the snake, and how well did it work?**

~ **How was your strategy for protecting yourself from this snake like your strategy for protecting yourself from threats in real life?**

~ **How does God fit into your protection strategy in real life? Explain.**

Say: **In this activity, you merely had to stay away from the snake—just one threat. Imagine all the threats God protects you from twenty-four hours a day, seven days a week! Today let's look at how God protected Paul from the bite of a venomous snake and learn about how God protects us as well.**

Exploring God's Word

Have students form four groups. Assign each group one of the following "characters" in Acts 28:1-6: Paul, the snake, Luke (the writer of Acts and Paul's companion), and the islanders. If you have a lot of students, you may want to add a fifth group and assign that group the part of sticks or fire.

Give each group a Bible, paper, and a pen or pencil. Have each group read the passage and then write a one-page account of the story from the perspective of its assigned character. Each account should contain the who, what, and where of the story, ending with the character's opinion of why Paul wasn't killed by the snakebite.

Allow groups about five minutes to prepare their eyewitness accounts. Then have one person from each group read his or her group's account (ending with Paul).

Then ask:

~ **What would your initial reaction have been to Paul's snakebite, had you personally witnessed it? Why?**

~ **How would you have reacted when Paul suffered no ill effects from the snakebite? Why?**

~ **Why do you think the islanders thought Paul was a criminal bitten as punishment?**

~ **Why do you think the islanders thought Paul was a god when he suffered no ill effects from the snakebite?**

~ **In what way was Paul's reaction to the snakebite an example for us of how we should respond to threats?**

~ **What does this story tell you about God's protection? Explain.**

Say: **Just as Paul's protection from the snakebite is pretty amazing, so is God's protection of us. God loved Paul deeply and loves you just as deeply. We should be**

Tell Me More

You may want to share this background information with your students to help them understand the story of Paul and the snake.

In Acts 23:11, God told Paul to testify about God in Rome just as he had in Jerusalem. The significance of this is that Paul could have confidence that he would live at least long enough to testify in Rome. None of us will lose our earthly lives until we have done what God has called us to do.

Paul was protected not only from the snakebite, but also from an angry mob that wanted to kill him (Acts 23) and from being killed in a shipwreck (Acts 27). Paul was even assured by an angel again, in Acts 27:21-25, that he would survive to stand trial before Caesar. God protected Paul until Paul's purpose and calling were complete. God holds every moment of our lives in his hands. He has a purpose and calling for each of us.

encouraged to know that God, as big and as awesome as he is, still takes time to watch over us and protect each of us individually.

Applying God's Word

Have students form pairs. Give each pair an item used for protection in some way (such as a helmet, a sword, steel-toed boots, football pads, a small piece of fence or wall, and shaving cream).

Say: **Think for a couple of minutes about how your item symbolizes a way God protects us.**

After a couple of minutes, have each pair present its item by answering the following questions.

Ask:

~ **How does your item symbolize a way God protects us? Explain.**

~ **When have you experienced or observed God's protection of someone in this way?**

Say: **I hate to think where I would be without God's protection from what is seen and unseen. I'm glad I don't have to anticipate and protect myself from all the threats that I could experience. I would much rather trust Almighty God, who knows all and sees all, to watch over me.**

Worship Time

Say: **Let's look at a psalm written by someone who understood just how much he needed God's loving care and protection.**

As a group, read aloud Psalm 144:1-2.

Ask:

~ **What was your first reaction to the words of this passage? Why?**

~ **Why do you think the psalmist would write a psalm like this? Explain.**

~ **When has God been your rock? your loving God? your fortress? your stronghold? your deliverer? your shield? your refuge? Explain.**

Tell students the following story.

Say: **Anya sat in the family car memorizing Bible verses. She was part of a junior high Bible quiz team, and that required knowing a part of one of the books of the Bible very well. Anya did this every week while her little brother, Zeek, had his piano lesson.**

The car was parked in front of the two-story house of the music teacher. Just before the lesson, Zeek told his mom, "I want Sissy to listen to my lesson." Mom reminded him that Anya needed the study time and that she had heard him practice. But Zeek was insistent. He went down to the car and returned with his big sister in tow.

The lesson began. Five minutes later the lesson was abruptly halted by a loud noise outside. Everyone stopped to watch a late-model car speeding away. The teacher's husband rushed in and exclaimed, "A gunshot...into the car...shattered the front passenger-side window!" The piano lesson was over. Everyone hurried down to look. Sure enough, there was the bullet lodged in the headrest, just where Anya's head had been five minutes earlier.

They all knew it immediately. God had used seven-year-old Zeek to save his sister's life. It was a profound moment. Zeek had responded when it didn't make sense to him or anyone else, and Anya had complied with his illogical request.

Two snipers were later arrested and sent to prison for five years.

Say: **Even miraculously, if necessary, God protects us from harm.**

Have students sing together a favorite chorus or song of praise, thanking God for his love and faithfulness.

Closing

Distribute cardboard, markers, masking tape, construction paper, and glue sticks. Have students work together using the distributed materials to create a symbol of God's protection over every aspect of their lives. (For example, they might create a big wall, a shield, or a coat of armor.) When students have created their symbol, have them write Psalm 144:1-2 in their own words on the middle of their symbol.

On the rest of the symbol, have each person write a prayer to God, asking for protection in a specific area of need. For example, a student struggling with a certain temptation may write, "God, protect me from myself and my desires." A student with an enemy who has threatened him or her could write, "God, protect me from my enemies, and give me wisdom to resolve this conflict peacefully."

When everyone has finished writing, ask:

~ **What is your initial reaction to the symbol of God's protection you created? Why?**

~ **What one aspect of God's protection are you most grateful for? Why?**

~ **Why did you choose to write what you did on this symbol of God's protection?**

Close by having students form pairs and share with their partners what each has written on the symbol of God's protection. Then have partners pray for each other according to what each has shared. End by praying the version of Psalm 144:1-2 that students have written on the symbol and by thanking God for his loving care and kindness toward you and the students.

Scripture Index

For more **amazing resources**

visit us at
group.com...

...or call us at
1-800-447-1070!

Group

Incredible things will happen